Raise to Release Endorsements

Not only are Victor and Esther godly parents passionate about raising and releasing children for the glory of God, but Victor is also a legend in student ministry. He has faithfully ministered to families, equipped teenagers, and served their parents. Their personal and ministry experiences combined with biblical wisdom and passion for the glory of God make *Raise to Release* a helpful and important book for parents.

—Eric Geiger,
Vice President LifeWay Christian Resources

This is an amazing and fresh approach on parenting. *Raised to Release* is a must read for parents, grandparents, and all those involved with students. It is true that the arrow, "our children, goes farther, straighter, and faster, when both mom and dad are holding the bow and pulling the string."

This is one of the freshest approaches to parenting I've read. The book is forged by a dynamic couple that has been most effective in student ministry and student counseling. No pun intended, this is one penetrating book.

—Dr Jay Strack
Founder and President of
Student Leadership University

Many Christian parents today look at the future for their children with more than a little fear. The world is changing rapidly before our eyes, moving farther from biblical truth and more into an abyss of moral relativism. My dear friends Victor and Esther Flores offer glorious hope to parents in this book! You will read about what really matters in parenting (and in life) from a couple who not only teaches this but also who have lived it out with their own children. Be encouraged! Be missional! Be actively helping your children live their lives to the glory of God.

—Alvin L. Reid,
Professor of Evangelism and Student Ministry/Bailey Smith Chair of Evangelism, Southeastern Baptist Theological Seminary

Victor and Esther have written a timely, must-read book that every Christian parent should read. This book is about God's expanding kingdom and how parents can join this mission of gospel advancement through our families.

—Steve Wright
Pastor of Discipleship and Church Planting,
Family Church, West Palm Beach

Oftentimes as Christian parents we fall into the trap of believing the goal of our parenting is to position our children to live the American dream. And often we are drowning in the chaotic ebb and flow of school schedules, extracurricular endeavors, and church activities. Multiply these schedules times however many children there may be, throw in a parent or two's vocational responsibilities, and you have a family going in several different directions. For those drowning in misplaced purpose and old-fashioned busyness, my friends Victor and Esther Flores have written *Raised to Release*. This book is a treatise on parenting written from the perspective of two parents who have simultaneously served in the trenches of student ministry for over thirty years. If you want to be the type of parent that is rich with purpose that enables a laser-like focus on the mission of God...then this book is for you.

—Brent Crowe, Ph.D.
Vice President of Student Leadership University and author of
Sacred Intent: Maximizing The Moments Of Your Life

Raise to Release is a God-focused, Spirit-led, and globally significant resource that every parent should read! As I have trained and mobilized students to make disciples of the nations for the last 20 years, I have often commented that we, the church, often focus on giving, praying, and going to be part of God's global purpose but that we were missing a critical piece—releasing. Victor and Esther guide us to consider this critical piece from their personal experience as parents and with the passionate commitment of years invested in discipling students and families. May God use this conversation to impact parents, students—and through them—the nations for His glory!

—**Melody Harper**
Department Chair & Assistant Professor
Global Studies Department
School of Divinity, Liberty University

From the introduction of the book, I was captured and drawn in. The personal stories by Esther and Victor made the pages of the book alive with warmth, love and transparency. The questions at the end of each chapter are excellent for study. This is a book that can be used as a manual for parents beginning their journey in fashioning their child, the arrow, to advance the message of our great God forward though their family. *Raise to Release* is a must read for all parents. It takes the role of the parents and puts it in a fresh new light.

—**Sammy Flores**
Palmetto Bay Campus Pastor
Christ Fellowship, Miami, Florida

In a culture where parents are teaching their children to fear culture, Victor and Esther Flores share great insight on how the Gospel can transform your children to world changers. The Flores' use of Scripture and truth will help parents see the value in who they are raising their children to love and serve. This book is thoughtful, creative and well written, I can't wait to give this book to parents in our ministry!

—**Jeff Borton,**
Pastor of Students Christ Fellowship Church Miami

RAISE
or RELEASE
[a Missional Mandate for Parents]

VICTOR FLORES
with ESTHER FLORES

LUCIDBOOKS

To Melanie, Tyler, and Julianna

CONTENTS

FOREWORD

Some of the Bible's most powerful and challenging words for parents are those of Psalm 127:4: "Like arrows in the hand of a warrior are the children of one's youth." Moms and dads have a natural and God-given inclination to protect and cherish our sons and daughters. Yet, our responsibility to nurture them can sometimes morph into an unhealthy fear and overprotectiveness. That fear, in turn, can cause us to hold our children back from fully following God's mission for their lives.

Like most parents, I need constant reminding that Jesus desires us not only to raise our children "in the nurture and admonition of the Lord" (Ephesians 6:4), but also to release them to serve the Lord wherever He calls them. That's why I'm so thankful that Victor and Esther Flores have written this wonderful book you hold in your hands.

In my years of ministry, I have never known any couple with a better personal understanding of what it means to bring up children to serve Christ. Victor and Esther have raised a son and two daughters—now all adults and married themselves—who love Jesus passionately and follow and serve Him daringly. Not only that, as long-term leaders in student ministry, Victor and Esther have rich experience in helping young people and their parents live missionally.

Raise to Release is filled with solid biblical teaching, real life examples, and practical steps of application to help parents take the journey of releasing their kids to make a difference for God's kingdom. I am thankful you're reading this book. Get ready for God to change your life through it!

Stephen Rummage, Ph.D.
Senior Pastor, Bell Shoals Baptist Church
Brandon, Florida

INTRODUCTION

Melanie, our first born, has always aspired to defy the status quo. Not because she was born with a thirst for being the trail blazer. In fact, she is like her dad— too often paralyzed by fear. Yet, in spite of these fears, she has always had a desire to push past perceived barriers. I remember a specific example when she was in middle school. Melanie tried out for her school's basketball team, an unlikely sport for her since she inherited her dad's height (I am 5'4"). She was so timid in her play. I can actually remember celebrating the first foul Melanie committed. Her mom and I marveled as Melanie proceeded to profusely apologize to the young lady she had just fouled.

My admiration for Melanie's tendency to attack her fears reached a new level after visiting her home one day while she was pregnant with her first child. While performing my daddy perfunctory duties—assuring Melanie that the baby's new nursery met my approval—I couldn't help but notice a hand-written phrase framed and strategically placed above the yet-to-be occupied baby crib. The penetrating words said,

Remember how the Psalmist described children? He said that they were as a heritage from the LORD, and that every man should be happy who had his quiver full of them. And what is a quiver full of but arrows? And what are arrows for but to shoot? So, with the strong arms of prayer, draw the bowstring back and let the arrows fly— all of them, straight at the Enemy's hosts.[1]

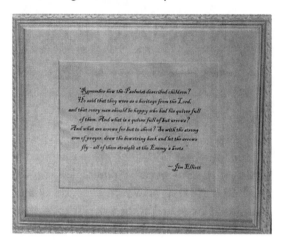

Even as a pastor, this was not what I expected to see above the crib of my soon-to-be-born first grandchild. The implications of this statement were staggering. Children like arrows? The weapon of a warrior? This image flew in the face of my long-held perception of what a good Christian family's purpose for raising a child should be. Yet there was something tremendously satisfying, God-glorifying about this unlikely baby dedication verse.

Melanie had found the quote in Elizabeth Elliot's book *Shadow of the Almighty: the Life and Testament of Jim Elliot.* Jim Elliot had written these words to his parents after telling them he was going to the mission field to work with a noted violent tribal community. He was referencing Psalm 127:3-5: "Behold, children are a heritage from the LORD, the fruit of the womb a reward. Like arrows in the hand of a warrior are the children of one's youth. Blessed is the man who fills his quiver with them!

He shall not be put to shame when he speaks with his enemies in the gate."

Jim Elliot was martyred in Ecuador on January 8, 1956.

The emotions of that moment beside my grandchild's crib have been transformative in my own family. To think that children are like arrows, given to us by our Creator, to raise and release! My experience as a student pastor had shown me that many times we follow a different prototype, one more akin to a raise and appease model. Yet my journey as a parent has confirmed the biblical accuracy of this raise and release model of parenting!

My wife, Esther, and I have been compelled by a clear call from God to magnify and amplify this radical, gospel-saturated and missional parenting model.

It is our humble conviction that in spite of the plethora of parenting models being regularly communicated, this idea of missional parenting could represent a fresh new wind.

It is our hope and prayer that serious consideration be given to adjusting our current convenient, pain-lessening, risk-reducing, success-positioning child rearing models. I appreciate the way John Piper expresses a similar thought:

> Woe to us if we ever become so fixated on the welfare of our own children that we lose our passion for rescuing lost neighbors and reaching lost nations. [2]

This is not a book about how to have a great family and raise great kids, but how to see our great God's message advanced through family!

There are two complimenting convictions that have fueled our passion for writing *Raise to Release*. First, we must respond to our King's command to make disciples who will, in turn, make disciples. Without a doubt, the mandate that Scripture gives parents is to disciple their children. 3 John 1:4 echoes what should be the passion of every Christ-adoring parent: "I have no greater joy than to hear that my children are walking in the truth." Did you get that? Not to marry well, have a good job, own a big house in the suburbs, or to live the American dream, but to walk in truth! And, of course, like any worthy accomplishment, we won't get that apart from a God-given plan. An arrow is most effective when fashioned correctly and accurately released to hit its intended target. How do you plan to fashion your children so that they will be accurately released with the greatest likelihood of hitting the intended target?

The second conviction that has fueled our passion for writing this book is that historically and biblically, young people are very often the tip of the spear in causing cultural change for the glory of God and the good of man. As we will see in later chapters, this is easily seen when we recognize that young people by their very nature are more easily shaped and sculpted and more willing to take risks stimulated by adventure. God works it that way and the enemy knows it. Parenting has much at stake—much more than we often realize. An honest appraisal of the current state of affairs among Christ-following families reveals a disturbing trend that is not new. The products of these homes are choosing a path devoid of the God they claim to know.

This book would not be complete without stressing the importance of admitting *Raise to Release* is necessitated by the fact that we are in a battle. Not a battle between parent and child, but between God and Satan—good and evil. To ignore this battle would be to our demise. We parents are warriors fashioning our arrow-children. We must go into this battle making much of the King and His Kingdom. Warriors must have unwavering allegiance to uphold this worthy King's cause, a clear, well-defined target, straight and true arrows, and focused vision. Our desire is to shape and send our children in such a way that we can echo with John, "I have no greater joy than to hear that my children are walking in the truth" (3 John 1:4).

The stakes are high. Our God-given mandate for parenting is clear: Love much, send out.

Psalm 127

UNLESS THE LORD
builds the house,
those who build it labor in vain.
UNLESS THE LORD
watches over the city,
the watchman stays awake in vain.
It is in vain that you rise up early
and go late to rest,
eating the bread of anxious toil;
for he gives to his beloved sleep.
Behold,
CHILDREN
are a heritage
FROM THE LORD,
the fruit of the womb
A REWARD.
LIKE ARROWS in the hand of a warrior
are the children of one's youth.
BLESSED
is the man
who fills his quiver with them!
He shall not be put to shame
when he speaks with his enemies in the gate.

BOOK ONE

THE WIN:
UNITY IN PURPOSE

1

UPHOLDING THE CAUSE
OF THE KING

I have very vivid memories of the births of our children that I will cherish forever. Specifically, I remember the moment when my tiny precious promulgators of future progeny were delivered and placed in my nervous but loving arms.

Do you remember what you felt when you first held your newborn? Did you feel relief, fear, or wonder? Maybe somewhere in there you may have thought, "There have been thousands of babies born today. But this one surpasses them all. She will have the best of the best that I can give her. The best opportunities, the best schools, the best parents. This is my chance to make all things right that I've ever made wrong."

Those thoughts of providing the best for your child may not have been the flood of exact musings and emotions you experienced at that moment. But if you are gut-level honest, you were probably thinking something close to that.

You might be thinking at this point, isn't wanting the best for my children a natural part of parenting? Shouldn't we want to provide a better life for them than we had and do our best to make that happen?

Unfortunately there is a slight flaw in this line of thinking. This minor miscalculation of ideas is not unlike what could be the adverse results of incorrectly entered coordinates into the Flight Management System of an airplane. What at first glance may appear as a slight error could over time be the difference between a safe arrival to your intended target of Whiporie, Australia versus a tragic landing in Whittier, Alaska.

Why would I say this line of thinking is flawed? Because it imagines and presumes an imprecise premise for parenting. In fact, if we parent from this perspective, we are writing the wrong story—a story without a happy ending.

Parenting, though no doubt charged with a huge responsibility, is only a chapter in the grand story of God. As with any story, we must go back to the beginning to fully understand its ending. And when raising our children, we must go back to the beginning of *the* story—the story of all stories—if we are to understand our role as parents.

The Greatest Story

In the Bible we read that God created the perfect environment for all to know and worship Him. In the midst of all this creative activity, angels were watching and praising God. They were His first creation. Lucifer, which means "bright morning star," was probably the most beautiful of all angels. He saw all others praising God, became jealous, then said in his heart, "I will ascend to heaven; above the stars of God I will set my throne on high; I will sit on the mount of assembly in the far reaches of the north; I will ascend above the heights of the clouds; I will make myself like the Most High" (Isa. 14:13-14). And thus ensued the greatest rebellion ever attempted, resulting in a third of the angels joining the revolt and the stain of sin inherited by God's crowning achievement—humanity.

In fulfilment of God's promised solution, as recorded in Genesis 3:15, God set into motion His rescue mission. Jesus, the perfect son of God, removed our sin through His death and resurrection and replaced it with His righteousness, thereby setting the captives free and restoring all to its former Glory. This rescue mission—which colors every page of the Bible as God's redemptive arc—manifests itself through the story of humanity's creation, fall, rescue, and restoration. This rescue mission can be defined by one word: *gospel*. The Bible is not just a collection of stories. It is *the* story of God. Every action of God has the same end, which is to increase the magnificence of God, and the gospel is the means. This story of redemption is not just for sinners to be saved, but the story keeps hearts adoring our Savior. It is an invitation to join God in His mission of rescue and restoration. Our aim is to daily understand, live out, and speak this gospel.

What does all this have to do with parenting? Everything! Without this premise as our foundation, the role of the parent will easily succumb to a culturally-shaped, me-centered child-rearing model. Yet, as warriors fighting for the fame of the name of our soon-coming King, we must have a warfare mentality and be gospel-centric in our mission. Parenting in this context is a rescue mission because we are in a battle!

The Essential Mission

God's divine design for us as parents is that we join Him in this global rescue mission of setting the captives free and bringing them into His forever family. God clarified this call from the beginning:

> I am the LORD; I have called you in righteousness; I will take you by the hand and keep you; I will give you as a covenant for the people, a light for the nations, to open the eyes that are blind, to bring out the prisoners from the

dungeon, from the prison those who sit in darkness (Isa. 42:6-7).

Jesus invites us to join Him in this cause:

The Spirit of the Lord is upon me, because he has anointed me to proclaim good news to the poor. He has sent me to proclaim liberty to the captives and recovering of sight to the blind, to set at liberty those who are oppressed, to proclaim the year of the Lord's favor (Luke 4:18-19).

His presence goes with us:

Go therefore and make disciples of all nations, baptizing them in the name of the Father and of the Son and of the Holy Spirit, teaching them to observe all that I have commanded you. And behold, I am with you always, to the end of the age (Matt. 28:19-20).

And, God's word reminds us that this plan of restoration will one day be complete:

Then I saw a new heaven and a new earth, for the first heaven and the first earth had passed away, and the sea was no more. And I saw a holy city, new Jerusalem, coming down out of heaven from God, prepared as a bride adorned for her husband. And I heard a loud voice from the throne saying, 'Behold the dwelling place of God is with man. He will dwell with them, and they will be his people, and God himself will be with them as their God. He will wipe away every tear from their eyes, and death shall be no more, neither shall there be mourning, no crying, nor pain anymore, for the former things have passed away.' And he who was seated on the throne said, 'Behold, I am making all things new.' Also he said, 'Write this down, for these words are trustworthy and true.' And he said to me, 'It is done! I am the Alpha and the Omega, the beginning and the end (Rev. 21:1-6a).

This promise was fulfilled in Christ, who was sent to do the Redeemer's work to overthrow the devil's kingdom and bring light and liberty to those who are separated from God with no hope!

The Glorious Alliance

Our parenting posture should be nothing less than establishing a military outpost-like family mindset where we lovingly and courageously submit to orders from our Commander in Chief. However, there is a celestial component in this battle unlike any other. A victory has already been declared. We are triumphant in Christ! Our adversary is a defeated foe. As soldiers of the Most High King, our rescue mission carries with it a glorious message that will echo into eternity. Christ has won! Paul describes it this way:

> But thanks be to God, who in Christ always leads us in triumphal procession, and through us spreads the fragrance of the knowledge of him everywhere. For we are the aroma of Christ to God among those who are being saved and among those who are perishing, to the one a fragrance from death to death, to the other a fragrance from life to life. Who is sufficient for these things? For we are not, like so many, peddlers of God's word, but as men of sincerity, as commissioned by God, in the sight of God we speak in Christ (2 Cor. 2:14-17).

A little later Paul reaffirms our responsibility as a Christ follower which, of course, includes parents:

> All this is from God, who through Christ reconciled us to himself and gave us the ministry of reconciliation; that is,

in Christ God was reconciling the world to himself, not
counting their trespasses against them, and entrusting
to us the message of reconciliation. Therefore, we are
ambassadors for Christ, God making his appeal through
us (2 Cor. 5:19-20a).

God has entrusted us with this great high calling of joining
Jesus in this rescue mission to restore all things by giving us
this ministry of reconciliation. There is no higher calling! And
as parents we are not exempt. When ("if" is not an option here)
our family is the conduit through which the gospel message is
released, the greatness of God will amplify the glory of God,
which is the target in parenting. Yet, while articulating such a
noble cause for prioritizing this lofty purpose for family, there
is no doubt the quick realization that it's not an easy task. In
other words, there will be opposition. There will be obstacles
and sorrows. We could all enumerate a thousand reasons
why, but the simple yet profound reality is this: we have an
adversary who is not of this world! The apostle Paul reminds
us, "Be sober-minded; be watchful. Your adversary the devil
prowls around like a roaring lion, seeking someone to devour"
(I Peter 5:8).

This fact is clear: parenting is a gospel-centric rescue
mission. Throughout Scripture, life on earth is characterized as
warfare. The Bible is replete with references to this effect. Why
else would Paul tell us in Ephesians 6 to put on the armor of
God? Or that "the weapons of our warfare are not of flesh but
have divine power to destroy strongholds" (2 Cor. 10:4)? To
young Timothy, Paul said, "Share in suffering as a good soldier
of Christ Jesus" (2 Tim. 2:3). Paul also told Timothy, "This
charge I entrust to you, Timothy, my child, in accordance with
the prophesies previously made about you, that by them you
may wage the good warfare." At the end of his life, Paul said, "I
have fought the good fight" (2 Tim. 4:7). We are invited to join
King Jesus in this same fight.

In fact, the gracious gift that God grants us by giving us children is His invitation to join forces with Him in His victory over sin, evil, and unbelief.

I'd like to take us back to the baby delivery room scene that I described earlier. We were not just giving birth to a child whom we hoped would have earthly significance. We were giving birth to a soldier-soul who will be strategically shaped by Christ-adoring, eternity-minded, warrior parents. Parenting is a missional endeavor.

> Missions is the divine activity of sending intermediaries, whether supernatural or human to speak or do God's will so that His purposes for judgement or redemption are furthered.[1]

Parenting and families are a means to an end. That end is worship. This is not a book about how to have a great family and raise great kids, but how to see the greatness of God advanced through our family.

Conclusion

We are in a battle. That precious bundle of joy that you held in the delivery room is like an arrow, not to coddle and caress and hold close to your chest or put on display near the family crest. Instead, you are to fashion and shape that arrow, to raise and release it in order to set the captives free and join the triumphant throng forever declaring the praises of our great King!

ACTION POINTS

1. Write one or two sentences from this chapter that help summarize what you've learned.

   _____

   _____

   _____

   _____

2. How does your acceptance of God's gospel and allegiance to the cause of the King affect the way you live?

   _____

   _____

   _____

   _____

3. How should this warfare mentality change the way you parent?

   _____

   _____

   _____

   _____

2

IDENTIFYING THE TARGET

Our son, Tyler, enjoys playing chess, one of the oldest and most popular strategy board games. The primary objective in chess is to capture, or checkmate, your opponent's king. The development of the game requires great focus and strategy. Impulsive moves will not likely result in the win, but it is important to quickly deploy your pieces to their optimal and safe posts. A knowledgeable player will want to control the center of the board and closely watch his opponent's development. This game of strategy is also one of sacrifice. The king is the most important piece of the board and every other piece can be sacrificed to save the king.

In the Old Testament, the one with all power and authority was always the king. In the New Testament, the faithful and true King that won the ultimate war and is gloriously coming back for His warriors is the Son of Man, Jesus! And "on his robe and on his thigh he has a name written, King of kings and Lord of lords" (Rev. 19:16). He is the only King deserving of our allegiance, and we gladly bow our knee to Him.

In parenting we must have a clear, well thought-out strategy in this battle and be willing to make sacrifices for the sake of the King's cause to "proclaim good news to the poor...proclaim liberty to the captives and recovering of sight to the blind, to set at liberty those who are oppressed, to proclaim the year of the Lord's favor" (Luke 4:18-19).

Someone Will Win or Lose

Our opponent's aim is to keep people confused and blind to a knowledge of truth. Much is at stake. We're talking about the difference between spending an eternity in the presence of our mighty and glorious King, or a thousand forevers in never-ending torment. When our arrow-children are sent out to local or foreign mission fields, we must be willing to sacrifice our small, temporal, self-advancing dreams for our children so that our King's eternal gospel-advancing mission can be realized all over the world. We must give our sons and daughters in order to gain fame for the glorious freedom message of the gospel. I believe this is what missionary Jim Elliot meant when he answered the question, "What are arrows for?" He replied, "And what are arrows for but to shoot? So, with the strong arms of prayer, draw the bowstring back and let the arrows fly—all of them, straight at the enemy's hosts." This, then, is the end goal of parenting. Inflicting damage on the enemy and his hosts with our arrow-children means hitting the target of God. He is the win. Consider these truths from Scripture:

> "This is eternal life," Jesus said, "that they know you the only true God, and Jesus Christ whom you have sent" (John 17:3).

> "You are my witnesses," declares the LORD, "and my servant whom I have chosen, that you may know and believe me and understand that I am he. Before me no

god was formed, nor shall there be any after me. I, I am
the LORD, and besides me there is no savior" (Isa. 43:10-
11).

An Indelible Impact

We parents pray that our children will know the infallible truth
of who God is and what He has done for us through the Bible.
The desire of our hearts is for our children to accept this eternal
God for themselves by admitting their need and personally
trusting in Jesus Christ to be their LORD and only Savior.
We also pray that they will love Him above all others and be
prepared and passionate about leading others to worship their
King and advance His rescue mission to restore all things.

To this end, the target we aim our arrow-children toward
is God. And God manifests Himself to us as the gospel. But
how does this gospel-target impact our parenting? How does
it impact our children? To answer these questions, we must
comprehend and embrace the richness of the gospel.

Our son, Tyler, blogged of his journey to understand the
gospel's implications:

> The gospel.
>
> I have been thinking a lot about the gospel recently.
> I'm not entirely sure what prompted this line of thought,
> but it's been months in processing, and I am just spending
> each day becoming more and more enthralled with the
> message and theme of the gospel.
>
> I take back what I said, I do know what prompted
> this: it was having to study and prepare for two separate
> lessons every week in addition to my personal quiet time.
> It seemed that no matter what I was reading, the theme
> seemed to come back to Christ and the gospel.
>
> On the one hand, the message of the gospel is simple.

The gospel is the message that we (the human race) offended a Holy God and by that rebellion incurred His just wrath. But God, because of His love for His own name and His love for us, sent His only Son to be the final sacrifice and substitution for us. On the cross He (God the Father) poured out His wrath on Jesus instead of us, completing the work of forgiveness. Three days later, Jesus rose from the dead, finishing the salvation work by breaking the barrier of death. Now we (that pesky human race again) have merely to "confess with our mouths that Jesus is LORD and believe in our hearts that God raised him from the dead, and we will be saved" (Rom. 10:9). And by saved I mean that our record of sin is erased and in its place, the righteousness of Christ is credited to us.

Somehow I feel like the words written in a small blurb to contain the message of salvation fall short of the full picture of the finished work of Christ. Of course, now that I think about it, I don't think that any words written down, short of the Holy Scriptures themselves, can capture the grandeur of the gospel. The gospel is the news that we were brought from death into life by the awesome blood of Jesus. And that life that we were brought into is so much more than we thought.

We thought that we bought ourselves a ticket into heaven. And when we reached the end of this life, we would wave our ticket around before some sort of heavenly gatekeeper, and thus our salvation would then come to fruition, ending in an eternity of golden streets and bright lights.

How dull.

Man, have we missed it. When did we make heaven the goal? As if some place could fulfill us just by our being there. We created in our minds a place beyond the clouds in which the very air reeked of happiness.

How insipid.

No. I will not accept that picture.

Fortunately for you and me that is *not* the true message of the gospel. The quickening of my soul to life by the blood of Christ happened both two thousand years ago and on the day that I confessed Jesus as LORD. That glorious day began a crazy journey that has no real end. My goal is Christ. My goal is to know Him completely and fully and by that knowledge gain Him.

The work of salvation is three-fold. We were declared right before God on the day that we surrendered to his Lordship. But then, the work of becoming more and more like him began in that same moment. Sanctification is the process whereby we, formerly alienated from our creator and coming groom, become more and more like Him.

And that is why I believe.

I have begun a journey toward my love that has had real ramifications in my life. There has been true change. He planted the seed of love in my heart, and I have been able to watch it grow. Oh praise His name! He is at work in my life, and the faith that I now possess is not a blind, mindless faith. It is a faith supported and buttressed by the work of Christ that I can see in my life. The final part of salvation is so vital. To be glorified and resurrected is more than just an end to the story. It is the true beginning of the real story that my heart has always been yearning for and is as yet unattainable while I wear this mortal shell. C.S. Lewis writes in *The Last Battle*,

> And for us this is the end of all the stories, and we can most truly say that they all lived happily ever after. But for them it was only the beginning of the

real story. All their life in this world and all their
adventures in Narnia had only been the cover and
the title page: now at last they were beginning
Chapter One of the Great Story which no one on
earth has read: which goes on forever: in which
every chapter is better than the one before.[1]

That is heaven. To know Christ. And isn't that the
gospel? To know Christ and to make him known?

Paul thought so. He said, "For to me to live is Christ,
and to die is gain" (Phil. 1:21). What was he gaining?
Christ.

Hello gospel.[2]

Indeed! This is the gospel: to know Christ and to make Him
known. We must give in order to gain.

A Strategic Movement

We should always be pointing our children toward this target
of treasuring Christ and "living for God's glory and the service
of their generation."[3] The object of our attention must be on
God's plan of salvation through the cross and its transforming
power to open eyes that are blind and to set captives free as
revealed in His living Word. Sending our arrow-children
through this God-ordained portal may mean exposing them
to the very front lines of battle. Our allegiance to the King
is what motivates us to love enough to sacrificially release
our arrows with intention. Notice that I did not say "to carry
our family name or to produce children who will care for our
aging bodies." That is a short-sighted, gospel-deficient goal.
Our five-second existence on this planet is but for one grand
purpose: gathering worshippers of the King from every tribe,
language, people, and nation to the praise of His glorious
grace.

He predestined us for adoption as sons through Jesus
Christ, according to the purpose of his will, to the praise of
his glorious grace, with which he has blessed us in the Beloved
(Eph. 1:5-6).

Conclusion

Jesus modeled this soul-satisfying, God-glorifying, faith-
multiplying process through His disciples. He made disciples
who made disciples. His disciples then launched the movement
to carry on His rescue mission. As parents, our purpose
mandated to us through Scripture is to be the primary discipler
of our children. Our children look to us for their foundation
and footing in this battle. As we shape our arrow-children
with the truth of God's word, we must daily mirror the gospel
message through unity with our partner in marriage. We are
always moving toward the target, that one grand purpose of
testifying of Christ and transforming the world. Warriors beget
warriors for God's global glory.

ACTION POINTS

1. Write one or two sentences from this chapter that help summarize what you've learned.

   _____

   _____

   _____

   _____

2. What do you think has been your target in parenting?

   _____

   _____

   _____

   _____

3. How does a gospel target impact parenting?

   _____

   _____

   _____

   _____

4. How does a gospel target impact children?

   _____

   _____

   _____

   _____

5. How does this rescue-mission mindset differ from
    typical parenting views?

    _____

    _____

    _____

    _____

BOOK TWO

THE WARRIORS:
UNITY IN PARTNERSHIP

3

ESTABLISHING A FOUNDATION

As a young married couple in Seminary, Esther and I were living very busy lives. I was a full-time student working two jobs. In the midst of this, we began anticipating raising a family. It became apparent that family needed to be a priority in spite of pressures. In fact, I can remember someone early on saying, "Victor, you can have the greatest ministry, but if you lose your family, you'll lose your ministry." Thus, our resolve became to prioritize our relationship with God first, then family, then ministry. Obviously, we've not always done the best with keeping our priorities straight. Nevertheless, raising a godly family has always been our hearts' desire.

God used many ways to get our attention so that we would realize the importance of family. One of the positions I held during those early years of marriage was that of Youth and Music Director at a very small church in Fort Worth, Texas. Esther and I regularly sang duets together. In fact, we still enjoy hilarious walks down memory lane during those rare moments when we view our VHS tapes. Our kids especially enjoy our 80's outfits! One of our personal favorites (and most requested) was "Household of Faith" by Steve Green.

Here we are at the start committing to each other
By His word and from our hearts
We will be a family in a house that will be a home
And with faith we'll build it strong

Chorus:
We'll build a household of faith
That together we can make
And when the strong winds blow it won't fall down
As one in Him we'll grow and the whole world will know
We are a household of faith

Now to be a family we've got to love each other
At any cost unselfishly
And our home must be a place that fully abounds with grace
A reflection of His face.[1]

When we first heard this song, Esther and I desired to build a godly family, even though we didn't know how. What we did know was that a strong marriage was absolutely essential and invariably foundational. God used Green's lyrics to reveal to us a clear message and its concurrence with Scripture that the foundation of the home must only and always be the LORD-ship of Jesus Christ.

An Upside-down Pursuit

Psalm 127:1 is the key to understanding this important truth: "Unless the Lord builds the house, those who build it labor in vain." When this psalm was written, God's people humbly asked for His help because the ruins of their city needed to be re-built and the fortress needed to be guarded. The phrase "unless the LORD" (Ps. 127:2) resonates loudly. He alone must build, inhabit, and expand the house. If the global glory of God through the spread of the fame of His name is the target, then to build a family on a foundation of anything other than Jesus is wasted toil! Practically speaking, this means that I purpose to prioritize the LORD-ship of Jesus in and with my family, beginning with my daily interactions with my spouse. This earthly relationship is the main stage to best model God-glorifying behavior in front of my children. The children that Jesus builds must begin with the house that Jesus builds! *Unless the LORD. . .*

When we live in a culture which prizes prestige, power, and possessions, a theology of weakness appears very contradictory and upside down. That's exactly the point. Jesus and His followers were always countercultural in their pursuits. We can do no different. We must say and stay with Paul's admonition in 2 Corinthians 12:9, "My grace is sufficient for you. For my power is made perfect in weakness." His worth and divine power is made known to us through our weakness!

LORD-ship begins with despair in myself: "Blessed are the poor in spirit, for theirs is the kingdom of heaven" (Matt. 5:3). I must admit helplessness. My life is not "do the best I can with God's help." I must see that this is not Christianity. Mark 8:35 says, "For whoever would save his life shall lose it, but whoever loses his life for my sake and the gospel's will find it." So this, then, is the heart of Christianity: I must hand over my life to the King (the good, bad, and the ugly) so that He can reveal to me how utterly worthy and satisfying He is. C.S. Lewis expresses it this way:

> Christ says, "Give me all. I don't want so much of your money and so much of your work—I want you. I have not come to torment your natural self, but to kill it. No half-measures are any good. I don't want to cut off a branch here and a branch there, I want to have the whole tree down. I don't want to drill the tooth, or crown it, or stop it, but to have it out. Hand over the whole natural self, all

the desires which you think innocent, as well as the ones you think wicked—the whole outfit. I will give you a new self instead. In fact I will give you Myself, My own will shall become yours."[2]

My daily resolve is to say, "Jesus, help me!" instead of "I got this!" My new life began at the Cross when I cried, "I need a Savior!" Every day this cry for help needs to be the same. This humble surrender to the King directly affects my marriage, family, and every other human relationship. These God-ordained relationships actually help me know Jesus better! We grow more devoted and dependent on Him through the difficulties. Then, together, we enter the battle for the cause of the King. This attitude results not in a *feeling* but in a *being* in Christ, *joining*, and *doing* of His mission.

The Fingerprints of Grace

We are not writing from a settled pursuit. There have been many wasted years of self-sufficient, self-serving, vain attempts to build our home. These periods rendered us useless to the mission of God. These failed attempts to build were direct results of pride: me making everything about myself, me having a large estimation of myself and my stuff. In other words, my pride makes me become a robber of the glory that God alone deserves! In the *Morning by Morning* devotional, author Charles H. Spurgeon, one of England's best-known preachers in the 19th century, reminds us,

> O believer, learn to reject pride, seeing that you have no ground for it. Whatever you are, you have nothing to make you proud. The more you have, the more you are in debt to God; and you should not be proud of that which renders you a debtor. Consider your origin; look back to what you would have been but for divine grace.[3]

Everything I am, everything I have, everything I do is because of this divine grace, and when I do live in humility (not thinking less of myself, but thinking of myself less), total dependence, and obedience to His LORD-ship, our family experiences times of greatest blessing. His fingerprints of grace were evident then and are evident now in the lives of our children.

Scripture reminds us to find our ultimate assurance in God and not in ourselves. Solomon writes in Psalm 127:2 that "it is in vain that you rise up early and go late to rest, eating the bread of anxious toil; for he gives to his beloved sleep." This passage reminds us to have restful confidence in His power and provision to build a strong foundation and fortress in our home. It is clear that alertness and work are not eliminated here on our part. We must, of course, faithfully labor on our marriage with all diligence in obedience, trusting that our labor is not in vain. The response that follows our belief that God is at work building our marriage and family is absent of restless anxiety. He is our strength and our protection. This is life and peace to its fullest degree because He is always at work!

In 1834, Edward Mote penned these words:

My hope is built on nothing less
Than Jesus' blood and righteousness;
I dare not trust the sweetest frame,
But wholly lean on Jesus' name.[4]

These words point a believer to the truth that Christ, alone, must be our Chief Cornerstone (see Isaiah 28:16; Psalms 118:22; I Peter 2:5-7; Acts 4:11; Ephesians 2:19-22). All our hope for our marriage and family is in Him. Our faith in God does not eliminate our questions, but we know where to take them!

Conclusion

The world and all of its wicked ways is all too quick to offer its temporarily satisfying, but deadly, substitute of child-rearing models. Trust me, the world beckons! The great theologian C.H. Spurgeon says it well:

> Hard earned is their food, scantily rationed, and scarcely ever sweetened, but perpetually smeared with sorrow; and all because they have no faith in God, and find no joy except in hoarding up the gold which is their only trust.[5]

All the prestige, power, or position the world promises will turn to wood, hay, and stubble. Yet, God has graciously given us the biblical blueprint we need to build a strong foundation based on His true cause which is to maximize the global glory of our King through our marriage and family!

ACTION POINTS

1. Write one or two sentences from this chapter that help summarize what you've learned.

   _____

   _____

   _____

   _____

   _____

2. Why does a theology of weakness appear to be an upside-down pursuit?

   _____

   _____

   _____

   _____

   _____

3. How does God show His kindness when we become utterly dependent on Him?

   _____

   _____

   _____

   _____

4. What ultimate assurance do we have when Christ is the foundation of our home?

_____

_____

_____

_____

_____

4

CONFORMING MY HEART

by Esther Flores

Whenever Victor is asked to officiate a wedding, he makes it a priority to individually address the bride and groom during the ceremony. He begins by saying, "Bill, the *best thing* you can do for Sally is to love God with all your heart, soul, mind, and strength. Sally, the *best thing* you can do for Bill is to love God with all your heart, soul, mind, and strength" (see Deuteronomy 6:5; Matthew 22:37; Mark 12:30-31; Luke 10:27). Our wedding vows reflect the covenant love of our King, and we respond and reflect this truth with each other. This is the foundation through which a God-honoring marriage is built. *Unless the LORD...*

During the years of our courtship, Victor and I recognized that our affection for one another had slowly replaced our affection for our Savior. We resolved to make Matthew 6:33 the theme for our relationship: "But seek first His Kingdom and His righteousness, and all these things will be added to you." Above all, I must pursue *Him*. I desperately need to seek the things of my King and His Kingdom as a priority over the things of the world. I desire to give my 100 percent in this battle to make Him famous in my home and through my marriage.

I will be speaking in the first person and using the singular form of "warrior" throughout most of this portion on marriage. I am fully aware that marriage is a partnership, but I am entirely convinced that no matter *who you are* married to, *who you are not* married to, past failures, past successes, imperfections—only one thing remains constant: God's perfect love. His love is complete, 100-percent perfection. I don't want my heart to be led astray from this breathtaking certainty. My devotion to the Supreme Lover of my soul must be simple and pure. Unrealistic and unfulfilled expectations for my spouse will always lead to disillusionment and discontentment in my marriage relationship. Once I've been in the arms of Jesus, no other arms will satisfy. The story of a Samaritan woman meeting Jesus for the first time at the well (John 4) leads to this conclusion: human arms just aren't long enough to reach my deepest needs. Ruth Bell Graham eloquently describes this truth:

> I pity the married couple who expect too much from one another. It is a foolish woman who expects her husband to be to her that which only Jesus Christ can be: always ready to forgive, totally understanding, unendingly patient, invariably tender and loving, unfailing in every area, anticipating every need, and making more than adequate provision. Such expectations put a man under an impossible strain.[1]

I read a book titled *Creative Counterpart* by Linda Dillow about 20 years ago that gave me such a fresh perspective for marriage. The pivotal section for me was fittingly named, "The Mystical Takeover." Upon completion of that book study, I announced to Victor that I had made a vow to God to find my worth and satisfaction in God alone. My new resolve was to no longer expect Victor to fulfill my deepest needs, and I would not pile mounds of pressure or guilt on him. No more manipulative games for my gain. Victor, as well, was charged with finding his ultimate worth and satisfaction in God only. My prayer echoed that of the psalmist, "Let me hear in the morning of your steadfast love, for in you I trust. Make me know the way I should go, for to you I lift up my soul. . .teach me to do your will, for you are my God! Let your good Spirit lead me on level ground!" (Ps. 143:8, 10). This focus became the posture of my heart instead of the idealistic expectations I had on my spouse. That was the day our marriage relationship began to take a whole new direction. We had found a new equation upon which to model and anchor our marriage.

This equation leads to a growing oneness with God, which in turn leads to a growing oneness with my spouse. This growing oneness with God takes time and obedience. It requires my faithful planting of the good seed that God does provide in His Word. This planting reminds me of a farmer sowing seeds in his garden. He takes special care and attention to the soil in which he planted. He can't control the weather, but trusts that God is able to give the increase even when winter comes. The seeds are safe and warm, growing slowly, deep under the cold winds and frozen surface. The result of the farmer's diligence and patience is a possible crop to feed his family. In the same way, I can't control all the circumstances of life. I must get good seed (from Scripture), faithfully plant and diligently care for the soil (my marriage), and trust that God's relentlessly planted truth, even in a frozen heart, will grow bountifully in His time and for His fame.

A victorious marriage that makes much of the King comes down to constant repentance from self and complete dependence on Him (God-awareness versus self-awareness). The life of any warrior should be one of allegiance, determination, discipline, and self-denial. My heart is daily being transformed and conformed to the image of my Lord and Savior. The following ten directives are foundational and have been accumulated through the years of this marriage-building process.

Wholly Depends on the King

This mandate can't be emphasized enough. It should be written entirely with a large font in capital letters!

Here's a challenge: read through the Old Testament of God's epic Story and count how many times His people grew independent, turned away from their One True King, yet still experienced victory and blessing. The answer? Zero. One such example is found in 2 Kings 17. This chapter records the downfall of Israel. Much light is shed on this very slippery slope—independence from God leads to dependence on self (or others). The Israelites wanted a God *plus* relationship. "So while these nations feared the LORD, they also served their idols; their children likewise and their grandchildren, as their fathers did, so they do to this day" (2 Kings 17:41 NASB).

Note the disobedience which led to defeat and death even after the LORD, in His grace, solemnly warned them. Wake up, warriors, when God records phrases like "did things secretly which were not right;…built for themselves in high places…set for themselves sacred pillars…did evil things…served idols… did not listen…rejected statutes…followed vanity and became vain" (2 Kings 17:9-15). Honor and thanks were stolen from God and put on the Israelites. What can we learn from their downfall? It is incumbent upon us to take heed and stay alert.

Anytime we, as the people of God, rely on someone or something else for our deepest joy and satisfaction, we are erecting self-made, modern day idols. These idols are not carved from stone or laden with gold but appear as good husbands, beautiful babies, impressive children, or perhaps in the unbalanced pursuit of sculpting our own body. You fill in the idol blank. It can be anything you take pleasure in above God. Remember from Psalm 127 that "we labor in vain unless the LORD builds" our marriage and family. Frustration, futility, and defeat will result in our self-centered, child-centered families. Where, then, is the victory of eternal value? The battle belongs to The King! A warrior depends on Him alone.

We need to heed this warning and gain wisdom from a warrior named King Hezekiah. He "did right in the sight of the LORD, according to all that his father David had done." He removed and broke down all their idols (2 Kings 18:1-4). He trusted in God. "For he clung to the LORD; he did not depart from following Him, but kept His commandments, which the LORD had commanded Moses. And the LORD was with him; wherever he went he prospered" (2 Kings 18:6-7). Hezekiah *clung* to the LORD. What a great word.

Hezekiah experienced victory at the beginning of his life because of his dependence on the King!

The heart of a warrior

Clearly Beholds the King

The sermon was titled "One Thing." I listened closely with conviction as our pastor taught on the story of Mary and Martha from Luke 11. The Holy Spirit gently reminded me that Martha (the very busy, distracted sister) was a picture of me. My conclusion at the end of that very convicting 30 minutes was, *there is only one thing that I must do each day: sit at the feet of my Savior.* Those words went deep into my core. I must look up from my agenda and consider God and His amazing story of redemption on a daily, even moment-by-moment, basis. I become what I behold. I advance what I admire. "Come to Me," Jesus says in Matthew 11:28.

The message that day left me with a new vision, a new resolve. He is a King worth fighting for.

The heart of a warrior

Securely Abides in the King

I am a list person. Whenever I read a methods book, I first peruse the summary looking for what I need to do to accomplish that particular task. I look forward to teaching my favorite part of speech, action verbs, to my second graders. In the game of charades it is easy to act out words like "come," "follow," "tell," or "stop." However, the verb "abide" may stump them. This single word has changed my whole perspective on *how* to have consistent Christ-centeredness in my marriage with my task-oriented, busy life. "Abide" is not a *do* word. It's a *be* word. We have a visual aid for this in John 15. This apostle must have been a visual learner like me.

To summarize, Jesus likened Himself to a grapevine with His Father being the master and cultivator of the vineyard. We are the branches on which the fruit is produced. If the branch does not remain connected to the vine, there is no fruit. The disconnected branch does not function for what it was created to do; instead, it is useless for its intended purpose to give recognition to the Owner of the vineyard. Jesus, the True Vine, is deeply rooted in holiness and provides the branches with the only means of holiness that produces the delicious, fragrant fruits of love, joy, peace, patience, kindness, goodness, faithfulness, gentleness, self-control (Gal. 5:22-23). Jesus says in John 15:4, "Abide in me, and I in you. As the branch cannot bear fruit by itself, unless it abides in the vine, neither can you, unless you abide in me." Branches don't strive to produce fruit—they simply remain connected. We cannot bear fruit without the sap! We have nothing within us of eternal significance without the life that God gives us through the Holy Spirit! Jesus says, "Apart from me you can do nothing" (John 15:5). The Master and Cultivator cares personally and is wise to know exactly what to do to make the branches fruitful. This may even involve the unpleasantness of pruning. The result of *abiding* is fruit that draws people in; they enjoy its benefits, and then desire to know who the Owner of the vineyard is. Who gets the spotlight (glory) when I display the fruit of the Spirit? Yes, God, in Christ, by His Spirit!

The heart of a warrior
Confidently Rests in the King

Try and visualize my father, mother, and five giddy girls traveling from a little town in central Pennsylvania to visit my oldest sister living in southern California. We were all crammed in a station wagon (the kind with wooden panels) hauling a very small Scotty travel trailer. We eagerly anticipated stopping at the KOA campgrounds each night where we feasted on Dinty Moore beef stew and experienced a below ground swimming pool. I had never seen a swimming pool like this! Daddy was the first one in. He held out his strong, capable arms and urged his little girl to jump. I had no hesitation. I jumped confidently because I knew he would catch me.

Today, I still find great happiness and relief when I jump into strong arms and follow a knowledgeable guide. I gain strength when I witness godly men and women follow their Savior. The one I now observe most closely is my lead warrior, my journey partner, Victor. He rises early every morning to behold God, admit his dependence, receive refreshment, and get his marching orders from the King. I thankfully follow his leadership in our marriage. This warrior's confidence is rooted in Isaiah 52. Verses 1-12 speaks of the deliverance of the Jews out of Babylon, which we, as rescued slaves from the enemy, can apply to the great liberty Christ has given to us. What joy and hope! Isaiah expresses the rejoicing and confidence we experience in the King when he writes, "For you shall not go out in haste, and you shall not go in flight, for the LORD will go before you, and the God of Israel will be your rear guard" (Isa. 52:12).

Restful confidence. What a great way to define trust. Warriors can believe this repeated message of the Bible: *God is able.* He is for us. He is with us. He is in us. The Psalmist writes, "For He gives to His beloved sleep" (Ps. 127:2). Our King reminds us over and over in His Word to fear not, because He knows. He sees. He cares. He keeps. I rest.

The heart of a warrior
Passionately Follows the King

I remember walking to the Statue of Liberty in New York City about 10 years ago. I despise large, crowded cities and battle with the fear of getting lost. Several factors gave me confidence and rest that day. First, my brother-in-law, Larry, was our guide. Second, he has a GPS built into his brain. Third, he had visited this city many times. With these components giving me confidence, all I needed to do was keep my eyes on his big plaid shirt. I followed as closely as I could. My footing was sure. The thought of running ahead of him never crossed my mind. When he turned right, I turned right. When he turned left, I turned left. When he stopped—yep, you guessed it. We arrived safely. Miss Liberty was stunning.

I am a warrior chosen by the King, holy (set apart for His service), and beloved (He is for me, not against me), according to Colossians 3:12. What a privilege to be adopted into a personal relationship with the King! This both breaks and encourages me to intentionally focus on and follow His marching orders, without running ahead. This honored life of a warrior requires allegiance and discipline. I must choose what my King chooses. I must value what He values. I must desire what He desires. *In my 10,000 steps today, LORD, my delight is to closely follow in Your steps.*

Warriors passionately follow whom they love and trust.

The heart of a warrior
Closely Imitates the King

I can remember daddy, after a short devotional from *The Daily Bread*, having all six of his daughters recite Ephesians 4:32: "Be ye kind one to another, tenderhearted, forgiving one another, even as God for Christ's sake hath forgiven you" (KJV). There was never much enthusiasm in my voice or desire in my heart; nevertheless, I said it. Now, as a second grade teacher, I lead my students to repeat from memory this same verse before we go to the playground. I ask the line leader each day, "So, why should we be kind, tenderhearted and forgiving, even when we don't feel like it?" Their rote response: "Because God is kind and forgives me!" Powerful truth here, one that must be applied to every human relationship as we closely imitate the King.

In marriage, it looks like this: kindness (when I don't feel like it), forgiveness (when they don't deserve it), speaking truth in love (when you want to scream it), patience (when you want your way), and gentleness—responding with goodness and self-control (silencing impulsive, hurtful comments)! Walter Wangerin writes,

> Forgiveness is a willing relinquishment of certain rights. The one sinned against chooses not to demand her rights of redress for the hurt she has suffered. She does not hold her spouse accountable for his sin, nor enforce a punishment upon him, nor exact a payment from him, as in "reparations." She does not make his life miserable in order to balance accounts for her own misery, though she might feel perfectly justified in doing so, tit for tat: "He deserves to be hurt as he hurt me." In this way (please note this carefully) she steps outside the systems of law; she steps into the world of mercy. She makes possible a whole new economy for their relationship: not the cold-blooded and killing machinery of rules, rights, and

privileges, but the tender and nourishing care of mercy, which always rejoices in the growth, not the guilt or the pain, of the other. This is sacrifice. To give up one's rights is to sacrifice something of one's self—something hard-fought-for in the world.[2]

What a foundational and captivating truth as we purpose to prioritize the Lordship of Jesus Christ in and with our family! Paul explains how we are to imitate the King in our marriage:

Put on then, as God's chosen ones, holy and beloved, compassionate hearts, kindness, humility, meekness, and patience, bearing with one another and, if one has a complaint against another, forgiving each other; as the Lord has forgiven you, so you also must forgive. And above all these put on love, which binds everything together in perfect harmony. And let the peace of Christ rule in your hearts, to which indeed you were called in one body. And be thankful. Let the word of Christ dwell in you richly, teaching and admonishing one another in all wisdom, singing psalms and hymns and spiritual songs, with thankfulness in your hearts to God. And whatever you do, in word or deed, do everything in the name of the Lord Jesus, giving thanks to God the Father through him (Col. 3:12-19).

I love this progression: a compassionate heart leads to kindness. Humility leads to meekness and patience which then leads to bearing with and forgiving each other (as I have been forgiven). Above all, I should love with the same measure with which He loved me, and the peace of God (harmony) will rule. I thankfully dwell in His Word. Why should I? For His glory and the good of my marriage which God designed to be a magnificent display of the gospel.

I will fight to emulate the King's supreme, divine, unique example. A warrior will bear His mark.

The heart of a warrior

Lovingly Surrenders to the King

As a little girl I would stand on my tippy toes trying to be taller than my sisters, dutifully singing the hymn "I Surrender All" by J.W. Van DeVenter:

All to Jesus, I surrender
All to Him I freely give.
I will ever love and trust Thee,
In Thy presence daily live.
I surrender all,
I surrender all.
All to Thee my precious Savior,
I surrender all.[3]

The pastor, my daddy, would be so proud of me. My tiny voice would echo against the wooden walls of our small church in Pennsylvania. I tried my hardest to sound like my beautiful mother, and failed miserably to harmonize with my older sisters. I was told that this song time was worship; yet at the time, Jesus had no worth to me. I had no deep desire to surrender any control over to Him. There were just too many rules to follow for my immature, rebellious heart.

This issue of control is what kept me dead in my sin and not surrendering my life to God until I was 17 years old. Even after I was married, I had a hard time surrendering to the LORDship of Christ because of this same sin of control, a lack of trust in God's sovereign plan.

When I was a young mother (and again recently as a young grandmother), I heard a sermon that challenged me to open up my tightfisted, controlling, selfish hands. Do I really know what is best for my children? I realized that I must give total surrender to the purposes of God for the lives of my family. This submission would require trust and a relinquishing of my control. I truly believe that this yielding to God's ways, which are so much higher than mine, is a daily decision. It is an opening of my hands in loving, submissive surrender every morning. During the sermon, the Holy Spirit reminded me that He deserves and delights in my trust. God alone can see what I cannot see and has complete control of what I cannot control. We win, not lose, when we surrender all to Jesus! In Matthew 10:39, our Savior says, "Whoever finds his life will lose it, and whoever loses his life for my sake will find it." Oh, how we miss out on experiencing the fullness of God's blessing when we hold so tightly to things or people in our lives!

My dependence and trust for God deepens as I spend time with Him. This relinquishing of *my way*, which leads to submission to *His will*, is a result of my growing love for Him. This surrender, an opening up of my tightfisted hands, is true worship. God is worth trusting.

This warrior accepts the challenge of living in selfless surrender. *All to Jesus I surrender, all to Him I freely give. I will ever love and trust Thee, in Thy presence daily live.* This is worship.

The heart of a warrior

Gratefully Fights for the King

It is with great gratitude that I join the mission of God: that every tribe, tongue, and nation would see Him as the King of Kings, personal Savior, and only true satisfaction. A warrior can't forget the gospel; indeed, the whole entire Bible is the gospel! To get the complete picture of this glorious truth, we must systematically read it over and over, Genesis to Revelation; but here are a few verses to get us on our knees:

For I delivered to you as of first importance what I also received: that Christ died for our sins in accordance with the Scriptures, that he was buried, that he was raised on the third day in accordance with the Scriptures (1 Cor. 15:3-4).

For our sake he made him to be sin who knew no sin, so that in him we might become the righteousness of God (2 Cor. 5:21).

He himself bore our sins in his body on the tree, that we might die to sin and live to righteousness. By his wounds you have been healed (I Peter 2:24).

And you were dead in the trespasses and sins in which you once walked, following the course of this world, following the prince of the power of the air, the spirit that is now at work in the sons of disobedience—among whom we all once lived in the passions of our flesh, carrying out the desires of the body and the mind, and were by nature children of wrath, like the rest of mankind. But God, being rich in mercy, because of the great love with which he loved us, even when we were dead in our trespasses, made us alive together with Christ—by grace you have been saved—and raised us up with him and seated us with him in the heavenly places in Christ Jesus, so that in the coming ages he might show the immeasurable riches of his grace in kindness toward us in Christ Jesus. For by grace you have been saved through faith. And this is not your own doing; it is the gift of God, not a result of works, so that no one may boast. For we are his workmanship, created in Christ Jesus for good works, which God prepared beforehand, that we should walk in them (Eph. 2:1-10).

I am the object of great grace! My two favorite words in the Bible are in Ephesians 2:4: "But God." As a daily reminder,

Victor and I display a sign right by our bedroom door with these transforming words. So with my beautiful and powerful companions named *Praise* and *Thanksgiving*, I fight on. These companions help this warrior fight the constant harassment of the enemy and distraction from the battle. *Praise* will always make me look up and give compliments to my King for who He is, and *Thanksgiving* will always remind me of what He has done. As I hold tightly to their hands, my whole perspective and attitude on life changes.

The heart of a warrior

Joyfully Serves the King

I learned a little chorus at Vacation Bible School when I was a child. Every year I teach it to my 8-year-old students with my ukulele. It's a simple song with an essential truth that helps us understand service for the King: correct priorities give correct motivation to serve.

Jesus and others and you, what a wonderful way to spell "joy."
Jesus and others and you, in the life of each girl and each boy.
"J" is for Jesus, for He has first place.
"O" is for others we meet face to face.
"Y" is for you, and whatever you do,
Put Jesus first and spell "joy!"

We follow the song with this little exercise. I say, "Vertical!" and my adorable students' arms go straight up.

They respond, "Love God!"

Then I say, "Horizontal!" and their arms go straight out to the side.

They respond, "Love others!"

My reply is, "Yes, children, our arm motions make the sign of the Cross."

This exercise illustrates a powerful truth. The vertical arm motion represents God's grace while the horizontal arm motion represents our extension of God's grace to others. The warrior who experiences the King's grace will gladly share that grace with others.

I joyfully serve.

Prayerfully Perseveres with the King

This morning, as I was waiting for Victor to return from his morning jog, I read 2 Corinthians 5-9. Chapter 6 is all about steady perseverance. My husband's discipline in physical exercise is a great picture of the spiritual truths in this chapter.

My loving, gracious, patient King gently reminded me once again to press on (Phil. 3:14) and "fight the good fight of faith" (1 Tim. 6:12). If the pursuit of the King and the extension of His Kingdom is my passion, then I must persevere in my communion with Him through prayer and in reading and studying His Word. We can begin by praying through the Lord's Prayer (Matt. 6: 9-13; Luke 11:2-4). Jesus models for his disciples in the following progression: first, we should adore the King and surrender to His Kingship. Next, we should admit utter dependence in His protection and provision. Finally, we must confess sin then thank Him for forgiveness and deliverance. Following this progression gets my mind off myself because I am praising Him then interceding for my husband, children, and others.

Remember the battle? Consider Paul's command in Ephesians 6:10-18:

> Finally, be strong in the Lord and in the strength of his might. Put on the whole armor of God, that you may be able to stand against the schemes of the devil. For we do not wrestle against flesh and blood, but against the rulers, against the authorities, against the cosmic powers over

this present darkness, against the spiritual forces of evil in the heavenly places. Therefore take up the whole armor of God, that you may be able to withstand in the evil day, and having done all, to stand firm. Stand therefore, having fastened on the belt of truth, and having put on the breastplate of righteousness, and, as shoes for your feet, having put on the readiness given by the gospel of peace. In all circumstances take up the shield of faith, with which you can extinguish all the flaming darts of the evil one; and take the helmet of salvation, and the sword of the Spirit, which is the word of God, praying at all times in the Spirit, with all prayer and supplication. To that end keep alert with all perseverance, making supplication for all the saints.

Paul emphasizes the importance of prayer and vigilance as we fight. Praying is like the oxygen I breathe and it fans the flame of love to my Savior. I experience more certain victories over the schemes of the enemy as I pray. I realize that simply saying a vow on my wedding day and having *determination* to follow Christ's example is not enough. Reflection of His covenant-keeping love in our marriage does not come naturally. It must be supernatural. I need to pray! We have an array of forces set against us as we walk through the wilderness of this world with our journey partners on our way to the Promised Land of heaven. We are not home yet.

I prayerfully persevere to display the covenant-keeping love between Christ and His people. I prayerfully persevere to show grace. I prayerfully persevere to mirror an attractive Gospel to others.

Conclusion

So, what do these personal ten directives have to do with marriage? Everything! Together in marriage we become fellow warriors, each giving our 100 percent by loving the King and His mission. We lock our shields, and, together in unity, raise and release our arrows.

Our prayer for establishing our family is echoed in this passage written by David: "Let the favor of the LORD our God be upon us, and establish the work of our hands upon us; yes, establish the work of our hands!" (Ps. 90:17).

I believe this should be obvious, but maybe it's not. In every human institution the key to success is solid leadership. The family is no different! Gospel-saturated leadership is a non-negotiable. Therefore, as goes the marriage, so goes the family. We are convinced that one of the parenting pillars in this "household of faith" is a God-infused, God-shaped marriage. It is this kind of unity that has the best chance of producing like-minded children that understand the scriptural admonition for every Christ follower (especially parents) to make disciples that, in turn, make other disciples. Like begets like! And in this style of parenting, that is a good thing—a God thing! Let's also not forget that this is our calling in the midst of a progressively God-denying culture. We must face facts: *we are at war for the souls of men in all nations, for the glory of God!*

ACTION POINTS

1. Write one or two sentences from this chapter that help summarize what you've learned.

    _____

    _____

    _____

    _____

    _____

2. What are some expectations that you have on your spouse that are humanly impossible for him/her to meet?

    _____

    _____

    _____

    _____

    _____

3. How do you react when the expectations are unfulfilled?

    _____

    _____

    _____

    _____

    _____

4. How can the statement, "The best thing you can do for your spouse is to love God with all your heart, soul, and strength," change the way you interact with your spouse?

_____

_____

_____

_____

_____

5. What are some ways your marriage reflects the gospel to your family?

_____

_____

_____

_____

6. What is the significance of parents having a united front?

_____

_____

_____

_____

7. What's the best way to become united with your
    journey partner?

    _____

    _____

    _____

    _____

    _____

8. Which of the ten directives mentioned in this chapter
    do you desire to mature in?

    _____

    _____

    _____

    _____

    _____

BOOK THREE

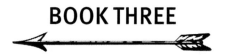

THE WEAPONS:
UNITY IN PARENTING

5

FASHIONING THE ARROWS

Not too long ago, I was in my assistant's office. On her counter was a bow and arrow prop used for a recent display. As I picked up the arrow, a myriad of thoughts began to run through my head because I had been marinating for some time about the premise for this book. As I lifted the arrow to study it more closely, it was obvious that an arrow is fashioned with a specific purpose in mind: to shoot at a specific target. While thinking deeply of the possibilities, a distinct thought occurred to me about what was clearly *not* a good use for an arrow—hugging and coddling! In fact, as I attempted to hold the arrow, the sharp edges of the tip gently poked my chest. And that's when the proverbial idea light bulb appeared above my head. Arrows work best when released. Likewise, children, brought up to fear the LORD, work best when released— not coddled closely to the chest forever. Of course, I am not suggesting we never hug or hold our children. On the contrary, expressing physical affection for children is indeed one of the ways in which we fashion our child-arrows.

To correctly understand the significance of children being likened to an arrow, we need to keep in mind the foundational mandate from our Savior to "go and make disciples" (Matt. 28:19). Are parents exempt from this command? Of course not. A parent's first and foremost allegiance, like that of all followers of Christ, is to King Jesus, second is to his or her spouse, and third is to his or her children. And it is their children with whom parents are charged to make disciples (who in turn will make disciples of their children).

Psalm 127:3 asserts that children are a heritage from God. That means children are a gift! They are not the fruit of man's labor, but a gift of God. The question we parents must answer is this: What will we do with these precious gifts to which we've been entrusted?

If we consider the description of children in Psalm 127:4 as we respond to this question, the implications are staggering. Psalms 127:4 explains that "like arrows in the hand of a warrior are the children of one's youth." Think of it: children like arrows! What are the ramifications of this verse? How does this comparison of children to arrows impact parenting and evangelism? How does this comparison bring glory to God?

If we closely inspect an arrow, we find that it is composed of four parts: the shaft, arrow, fletching, and nock. By examining each of these four components, we can draw parallels to how we as parents can raise our children for maximum world impact to the glory of God.

The Shaft: The Identification of Truth

"Shaft: the body or stem of an arrow" (Merriam-Webster Dictionary)

According to *Encyclopedia Brittanica*, the access vault of all information, the arrow predates history.[1] Yes, arrows have been around awhile. What originally insured the accuracy of the early warrior's arrow was the straightness or trueness of the hand-hewn stick, or shaft, portion of the arrow. There were no high-precision, computer-driven cutting tools back then! It was up to the warrior to search out the straightest sticks he could find in order to make his arrows. He knew lives were at stake. Finding and fashioning the straightest arrows, his prime offensive weapon and means of protection and provision, was not something he took lightly.

Today, not much has changed with regard to the most basic component of an arrow. The straightness or trueness of the shaft is still a major factor in determining the accuracy of the arrow's flight. No true shaft means no true flight.

One of the reasons the shaft is so critical in determining the flight of the arrow is that the shaft is the piece to which all the other components of the arrow are connected. These components, held together by the shaft, are essential to the arrow's function and accuracy in flight. Just as the shaft of an arrow is the greatest determiner of the accuracy of the arrow's destination, so truth—the Word of God—integrated by parents into the life of a child will be the greatest influence in the ultimate destination of a child. The Word of God is the one constant that will hold all child-rearing components together. In John 14:6 we read that "Jesus said . . . I am the way, and the truth, and the life. No one comes to the Father except through me." Every truth-based action and attitude fashioned into your child should be based on the words of the Author of Truth. His Words will direct the flight and landing place of your child.

Although there will be outside forces lending their voices, dear parent, please know that in spite of the fact that some of these voices at times are shouting very attractive sounding words, they do not (yes, get this: they *do not*) possess the proximity you possess as parent to pass on *your* influence. Much research to date, both secular and sacred, has come to the same conclusion with regard to which voice speaks the loudest and penetrates the furthest in this ultimate shaping and sculpting of children. It is that of the parent! *You* are the number one influencer! This is why it is imperative that you find your sustenance for survival in the Word of God. Proverbs 30:5 promises us that "every good word of God proves true; he is a shield to those who take refuge in him." Not only will His Word be your shield and refuge; it will also equip you to be the instrument of instruction and influence in shaping your child. As parents, our number one responsibility is to grow in the likeness of Christ, and thereby pass on this same likeness to our children, who will in turn pass on this same likeness to their children. We call this making disciples that make disciples. It is the number one command given to all Christ followers, especially parents.

Again, though this may seem obvious, because of its importance it bears repeating: the only God-glorifying means of raising an arrow who will inflict damage to the forces of darkness is to insure the intentional transfer of truth from the Author and Person of truth, Jesus Christ. Parents, you can't fake this one. Once the arrow is released, the trueness of its flight undoubtedly will reveal who its Master and Maker is.

Three very familiar and helpful parenting principles follow:

1. You can't pass on what you don't possess.
   If you as a parent are not daily orienting your life around the changeless truths of God's Word, it's not likely that your children will.

2. More is caught than taught.
   Those little eyes are watching you.

3. Take the time to tell them the truth.
   Digest and display the gospel by reading His Word each day.

It is the straightness of the arrow which most influences the strength of the arrow. In a similar manner, it is the truth of the

Word of God that will strengthen our children and equip them to overcome the enemy. We are reminded of this exhortation in 1 John 2:14: "I write to you, fathers, because you know him who is from the beginning. I write to you, young men, because you are strong, and the word of God abides in you, and you have overcome the evil one."

At this point we need to acknowledge that a great archer can possess the best archery equipment possible, yet unforeseen circumstances can occur upon release of the arrow which will cause the flight of the arrow to be somehow disrupted. As every parent can attest, perfect parenting skills (if there are such things) are no guarantee of perfect children. Yet our sovereign God will always work His perfect plan.

Perfect parents don't produce perfect children, especially since that was never the plan. God's perfectly planned purposes will prevail for the good of man and ultimate global glory of God. Notice that I said God's plans, which are always "plan A" plans.

There will be those instances when God's plan for my family, from my vantage point, will resemble a rock-filled, pot-hole littered detour instead of the beautifully-manicured, artfully-designed, rest stop-punctuated interstate highway. All of us have known God-adoring parents who did it right, yet the trajectory of their child's life has gone way off course with very little resemblance to the likeness of Christ.

In like manner, I could recount to you example after example of students who have been active participants in our student ministry who have greatly impacted the Kingdom as an unapologetic disciple of Christ. Yet, they did so apart from God-exalting parents. There will always be that humanly undiscernible, sovereign plan of God which will always prevail according to His good pleasure! As a Christ-following parent this should be a peace-producing imperative: trust God as you tell them the truth!

Our admonition at this point is to encourage parents with

the reminder that they continue to pursue their number one responsibility as a parent—keep passionately loving the Savior and redemptively relate to their children! It is precisely during these times of despair as our children wander that the truth of the Gospel is most beautifully displayed. His truth wins! His faithfulness has demonstrated throughout history and will continue to bring "beauty for ashes, joy for mourning and a garment of praise instead of a spirit of despair" (Isa. 61:3).

Our rest comes in the faithfulness of the Builder. To reiterate what the Psalmist said, "Unless the LORD builds the house, those who build it labor in vain. Unless the LORD watches over the city, the watchman stays awake in vain. It is in vain that you rise up early and go late to rest, eating the bread of anxious toil; for he gives his beloved sleep" (Ps. 127:1-2).

While there is no shortage of parent-pleasing, child-appeasing instructional manuals, there is only one true manual which will equip us to raise our children to impact eternity. In revisiting our passage from Psalms which provides us with the fitting image of children likened to arrows, we must ask ourselves the same question Jim Elliot asked: "What are arrows for?" The answer and its implications cannot be ignored. As the purpose of the arrow is to release and impact, so is the divinely ordained purpose of children: to raise and release for the spread of the fame of our King!

As parents, we have no greater ally in the shaping of our arrows than the Word of God. Colossians 3:16 encourages us to "let the word of Christ dwell in you richly, teaching and admonishing one another in all wisdom, singing psalms and hymns and spiritual songs, with thankfulness in your hearts to God." It is this Word richly dwelling within us and our children that will most equip our children for their flight once released. With any arrow, the stronger the shaft, the less it will bend. Penetrating culture with the Gospel message requires remarkable strength and resolve. Our desire for our children, given to us by our Savior, is that they transform culture rather than conform to it (Romans 12). It is only with and by the Word of God that life-change for the glory of God can happen!

The quintessential Bible passage which speaks specifically to the spiritual armor for every Christ-follower is found in Ephesians 6:10-16 and is of great help to us here. The section of armor I would like us to zoom in on is the belt of truth mentioned in verse 14. The belt for the Roman soldier served as the anchor point which held his meal kit, sword, and canteen. This same belt prevented the soldier's armor from shifting in battle. Once again, we are reminded of the vital anchoring role that truth, God's word, accomplishes in the life of a believer, which, like the straight and strong shaft of an arrow, is highly influential in the outcome of the battle. I don't believe we can say too much about the importance of our children anchoring their lives on scripture, learning both *what* to think and *how* to think (developing a Christian worldview) in preparation for this earthly battlefield.

The Arrowhead: The Penetration of Truth

"Arrowhead: a piece of stone or metal that forms the point of an arrow" (Merriam-Webster's Dictionary)

In the 2001 movie *Pearl Harbor*, there is a scene toward the end of the movie where the main character, Captain Rafe McCawley, is talking with Lt. Red Winkle. As they are discussing the dangerous mission they are about to undertake in retaliation of Japan's attack on Pearl Harbor and their role in it, Red says, "We're the tip of the spear, Rafe!" Red is passionately implying that Rafe and Red will be the first ones to go in and prepare the way for the rest of the force to do its job.

So what does this story mean for us as parents?

The tip of the spear and an arrowhead are designed to pierce and impact. In a similar manner, we read in Hebrews

4:12 that "the word of God is living and active, sharper than any two-edged sword, piercing to the division of soul and of spirit, of joints and of marrow, and discerning the thoughts and intentions of the heart," God's Word has the power to pierce and impact. As Christian parents, we pray that our children will know and live the power of God's Word. We pray that they would experience this as they speak and share His Word to penetrate and push back darkness.

God's Word also has the power to leave a lasting mark. And if you choose to leave a mark on your child through teaching and praying scripture over your child, this will determine the mark he or she will leave on this world.

If we were to conduct an informal poll of a random sampling of parents and ask them if it is their desire that their children leave a mark on this world, the response would be high in the affirmative. This of course begs the question, "Mark for what?" Their *children's* fame and glory? That their *children's* names would be remembered? As followers of the King of Kings, personal fame and glory would belittle the *only* One worthy of fame and glory!

As a student pastor for more than 30 years, a familiar point of contention and controversy between well-meaning Christian parents and their children is how to respond to wayward behavior when the question of the sincerity of a salvation experience surfaces. Typically this is how the scene will play out: the child professes Christ at a young age, but as a teen begins to show signs of rebellion. Parents, assuming the child's salvation is secure, look for ways to deal with rebellious behavior and attack what is often a symptom of the actual problem. Too often, salvation never occurred. There was no real point of Gospel penetration—only behavior modification. It is not enough to identify the truth (demons believe and shudder, James 2:19); there must be acceptance of the Truth (I am the Way, the Truth and the Life, John 14:6). There must be a distinct point in time when this person surrendered his or her life to Christ. This may seem so very obvious, yet it is so very common. Parents, distraught by the godless behavior of their assumed born-again child, apply ineffective corrective measures. Unless our children have been marked by the Gospel, and unless their lives have been irreversibly transformed by the Gospel of Jesus Christ, there exists no hope for them to leave a mark on this world for the cause of our King!

As a warrior-parent mirroring Psalm 127, my desire as a parent is to raise and release my Gospel-marked child in such a way that he or she has a resolute commitment to not rest until others are marked and forever changed by this same Gospel.

As Christ-adoring parents, our desire for our children is to leave a mark, provided that mark has a striking resemblance to the King of Glory! A source of great encouragement to me, and—I believe—a vital responsibility of all Christian dads, is to read the stories of the great saints of old. One such powerful story has been that of Jim Elliot and his four companions who were murdered by native Ecuadorian Indians while seeking to win the natives to Christ. Although this tragic incident occurred in 1956, echoes of this story continue to reverberate and fuel the cause of Christ! Without a doubt, this story has left an indelible mark inspiring all who seek to take this life-changing message of Jesus Christ to the ends of the earth.

In his thoughtful but poignant reply to his mother, Jim Elliot asked the question referencing the Psalmist: "What are arrows for?" Let's revisit this important quote from which the premise of this book is derived:

I do not wonder that you were saddened at the word of my going to South America. This is nothing else than what the Lord Jesus warned us of when He told the disciples that they must become so infatuated with the kingdom and following Him that all other allegiances must become as though they were not.

And He never excluded the family tie. In fact, those loves which we regard as closest, He told us must become as hate in comparison with our desires to uphold His cause. Grieve not, then, if your sons seem to desert you, but rejoice, rather, seeing the will of God done gladly.

Remember how the Psalmist described children? He said that they were as a heritage from the Lord, and that every man should be happy who had his quiver full of them. And what is a quiver full of but arrows?

And what are arrows for but to shoot? So, with the strong arms of prayer, draw the bowstring back and let the arrows fly—all of them, straight at the Enemy's hosts.[2]

As I shared in our introduction, it is Elliot's response to his concerned parents prior to his going to the jungles of Ecuador as a missionary from which Esther and I find our inspiration for this book. God in His wondrous wisdom is still using the faithfulness of these servants to inspire others to dedicate their lives to help take the message of the gospel to unreached people groups all around the world. I share this reminder in order to make this point: Our parenting practice must bear this mark of Jesus' command to go and make disciples at whatever the cost! We must ask ourselves, *Am I shaping and sculpting this arrow, this child, in such a way that, once released, he or she will go with fearless commitment to whatever Christ calls for the sake of the Gospel?*

The consequence of Elliot's choice to go where Christ called is still bearing its mark! When I think about the power of the gospel eternally penetrating, especially as it relates to the story of Jim Elliot, there are several distinct marks that emerge for me. One of them is the story of Steve Saint.

Joni Eareckson Tada explains that Steve was five years old

when his dad, Nate Saint, was killed along with Jim Elliot and three other missionaries in January of 1956. Since that day, relatives of both Elliot and Saint have returned to this tribe. Through their gospel-saturated lives and faithful obedience to go where God directs, the Waodani, also known as "Auca" (meaning naked savage), have been largely converted to Christ! But the most compelling piece of this story which highlights the irreversible power of the gospel to leave its undeniable mark is the loving relationship that has developed and deepened between Steve and Mincaye, the Auca warrior who actually delivered the final spear that ultimately killed Nate Saint, Steve's dad. The relationship that exists today between Steve and Mincaye can only be explained by the power of the gospel to penetrate and transform lives.[3]

Our arrow-children will leave a mark. What will that mark be? How can we as parents provide the proper environment that will help shape and mold our children into cunning warriors for Christ upon release, with some even going where the Gospel is not yet preached?

The Fletching: The Stabilization of Truth

"Fletching: the feathers on an arrow; also: the arrangement of such feathers" (Merriam-Webster's Dictionary).

I've never shot a real arrow, but as a child I've enjoyed the thrill of letting my imagination run wild with thoughts of piercing a wild animal or some fictional villainous character with one of those cool fake arrows with that suction cup arrowhead. Not very impressive, I know. In fact, if you had asked me three months ago, "What is a fletching?" I may have responded with, "You want me to fetch what?" And at this point, if were it not for our dear friend, *Merriam-Webster's Dictionary*, I'd still be completely clueless. Yet with the initial germination of our arrow-based, raise-to-release idea as a missional parenting model, our appreciation for the depth and richness of this analogy has grown considerably.

As I learned from the Trueflight Feathers Fletching Guide, fletching is found at the back of an arrow and is used for stabilization. The fletching acts as airfoils to provide a small amount of force in order to increase stability. It is designed to help the arrow stay pointed in the direction of its travel.[4] I'm certain by now you are already thinking of how this might translate in discussing the analogous pieces to child rearing.

We've already stated how an arrow whose shaft is straight and true will have greater likelihood of hitting its intended target than an arrow with a bent shaft. Likewise, children who are shaped by the straight and true Word of God will have the best chance of hitting the target. We are again reminded in God's word to "sanctify them in the truth; your word is truth" (John 17:17).

We've also discussed the importance of how the arrowhead will strike the target first and leave its mark. In similar manner, God's truth should be the first impact upon our children which will in turn leave a mark upon their lives. We're encouraged in Philippians 2:2 to "make my joy complete by being of the same mind, maintaining the same love, united in spirit, intent on one purpose" (NASB). We're asked the question, *What Christ-honoring mark do we want our Christ-filled children to leave in a Christ-less culture?*

As we look at the fletching of the arrow, I would like to propose the following lesson that I believe will provide a powerful parenting help. Whenever natural fletching is used, the feathers on any one arrow must come from the same side of the bird. The slight twist in natural feathers then makes the arrow rotate in flight which increases accuracy. Misaligned arrows thwart true flight. Taking into consideration that we've already established how parents are the number one influencer in the lives of their children, consider how important it must be for Christ-adoring parents to be *united* in applying Gospel-saturated parenting principles. A sure deterrent to disrupting the flight path of your arrow-child will be the conflicting messages coming from the most influential sources!

The Nock: The Connection of Truth

"Nock: one of the notches cut in either of two tips of horn fastened on the ends of a bow or in the bow itself for holding the string" (Merriam-Webster's Dictionary).

The nock holds the arrow in position on the string when the bow is drawn for firing. In order for the arrow to hit its target, the nock must be precisely aligned with the bowstring. This connection is critical. To be sure, the key to the maximum effectiveness of the nock is precision alignment and placement of the bowstring in the nock. Every skill, as well as each piece of equipment and hour of practice, will be at the mercy of the execution of this critical step. This step is the final action taken before the actual release of the arrow.

So let's turn a corner here. What is the parallel between the nock and parenting?

In any healthy, Christ-imitating, parent-child relationship, there must be a clear heart connection. And that heart connection will be established by and extended through that precious commodity we call time! In any book or writing about strengthening human relationships, spending time together is a non-negotiable. And this is especially true with the parent-child relationship. Check yourself. How is your heart connection today with your child? Below average, average, above average?

Consider also how this heart connection with your child will have direct bearing upon the unavoidable transitional events when actual release (letting go) occurs. Three biggies include bidding good-bye to a child leaving home, giving your child away in marriage, and sharing final farewells at a deathbed. The extent to which you, the parent, have invested time in connecting with and feeding this relationship with your child will be commensurate with the beauty and satisfaction that will occur at these pivotal points of transitional release.

In talking with parents about parent-child relationships, I like to ask parents to use their imagination and fast forward in time to one of these very real transitional releases. What is your desire as a parent for these moments? Will these moments be filled with God-honoring, exceedingly great joy and satisfaction? Or will these moments be filled with regret? Beginning with the end in mind helps us realize the implications of our actions.

So what does all this have to do with an arrow nock? In order for the actual release of the arrow to occur with the most accuracy-inducing action possible, there 'must be a precision fit between the bowstring and arrow nock. Every preceding step must be commensurately prioritized and skillfully executed. In the case of parenting, your excessive joy upon the transitional release of your child will be predicated by the extent to which you prioritize the abiding in Christ in the life of your child.

We believe this biblical imagery of children as arrows, an offensive weapon designed to hit and penetrate its target, is not the typical view we have of our children. Working within the framework of this viewpoint, how do we—warrior parents—disciple and mentor our children in such a way that they will, through their Gospel-saturated lives, inflict the most damage possible to the kingdom of darkness? How do we as parents bring "many sons to glory?" (Heb. 2:10).

To be sure, every Christ follower is commanded to make disciples. As Jim Putman and Bobby Harrington explain, a disciple "is a person who follows Jesus, is transformed by Jesus and joins Jesus on His mission."[5] Just as Paul wrote that "faithful men" are to in turn "teach others," we are to do the same (2

Tim. 2:2). In other words, a disciple makes disciples who makes disciples.

Conclusion

We believe any measure of parenting effectiveness that does not purpose as its first priority to make disciples who make disciples is biblically inaccurate and tragically misdirected. After many years of serving as a student pastor in both small and large churches, my resolve to promote the power of gospel-centric parenting to raise and release remains undiminished.

As we move further along in our book, we will provide practical tools, suggestions, and helps for you, the parent, on ways to shape and sculpt your arrow-child that they may have the most accurate release and flight possible with the greatest likelihood of hitting the intended Christ-ordained target. Our prayer is that the following chapters will encourage and equip you to disciple your precious arrow-children and direct their path to align with the mission of God.

ACTION POINTS

1. Write one or two sentences from this chapter that help summarize what you've learned.

   _____

   _____

   _____

   _____

   _____

2. What are some ways young warrior-parents can prepare to raise and release their arrow-children?

   _____

   _____

   _____

   _____

   _____

3. How has the truth of God's gospel shaped and strengthened you?

   _____

   _____

   _____

   _____

   _____

Have you ever shared this with your children?

_____

_____

_____

_____

_____

4. When do you tend to have the best faith-related, heart-connecting conversations with your children?

_____

_____

_____

_____

_____

5. As you imitate Jesus and disciple your children this week, what can you do to direct their path to align with the mission of God?

_____

_____

_____

_____

_____

6

GUARDING THE DEPOSIT

by Esther Flores

During our first year of marriage, Victor held the position of security guard on our college campus. As part of his basic job description, he was to guard, patrol, and monitor the premises to prevent theft, violence, and rule infractions. Victor also was assigned the task of authorizing entrance and departure of employees, visitors, and students.

In a similar manner, we warrior parents are charged with this same account of responsibilities. Our premise to possess Christ and pass on His promises is not a passive endeavor! The apostle Paul exhorts his young protégé to flee from evil, follow after Jesus, fight for faith, and be faithful to love God above all else. He concludes by stating, "O Timothy, guard the deposit entrusted to you" (1 Tim. 6:20). Paul again restates, "By the Holy Spirit who dwells within us, guard the good deposit entrusted to you" (2 Tim. 1:14). All of these admonitions involve commitment to truth and action.

Stay Alert

The precious treasure of the true, entire gospel must be guarded with all diligence within the walls of our home. With the strength of the Holy Spirit, we must stay alert, watching for any areas of vulnerability of sin in the shelter where our children long to feel safe.

The world has depraved minds which undermine the worth and truth of Scripture everywhere we turn. We must have the courage to avoid any form of corruption or mixed messages. Persevere, dear warrior, when your children beg for compromise. Welcome your children's *why* questions and carefully give answers based on Scripture. We must set boundaries and reject anything that God hates and not be careless or negligent in our duty. Keep a careful watch.

Our granddaughter, Elianna, has many food allergies. Her mommy lovingly prepares special meals, carefully reads labels on all food products, and unapologetically asks many questions about ingredients and food preparation when the family goes to restaurants. Her protection and provision for Ellie's health should mirror our concern when it comes to the rejection of any form of impurity coming into our children's minds and in our home. Since we have been entrusted with this precious deposit of God's truth, we must relentlessly and tirelessly stand on the watch tower. Jesus Christ says in His Word that "the thief comes only to steal and kill and destroy. I came that they may have life and have it abundantly" (John 10:10).

Monitor the Premises

The enemy invades, seizes, and carries away the affections of our children. Warriors guarding the good deposit of truth must monitor closely what comes into our home in this digital age in which we live. This generation has unlimited exposure and interacts habitually with modern technology. As a teacher, I recognize the value of the internet and the variety of resources for students to develop hand-eye coordination, learning strategies, creative stimulation, and information about our world. We must be purposeful, not detrimental, with the use of the amazing technologies of our time. Parents—and not social media websites—still need to be the primary source of guidance and information for children. As guards on the watch tower, we need to monitor the premises to prevent theft. We must be careful not to let these electronic devices steal time with our families. If we are not prudent, their overuse can become a major enemy to relationships with our spouses and children. We need to set limits and set an example of balance! Family is the quintessential firewall. Decide on a healthy amount of phone and screen time for yourself and your children. Bring everyone onboard with this decision and discuss it together with the whole family giving input. This exercise of control may aid in the avoidance of conflict and arguments about the amount of time one was spending online. Maybe for one whole day, hide your phones! Make it a priority to connect intentionally with your family during sustained face-to-face conversations, long walks, and engaged connection and enjoyment of God's creation. Go through the day looking for His fingerprints! Be present. Spend time laughing and playing with one another and instill a heart for Jesus. Be all there.

Authorize Entrance

The thief will also kill and destroy through false doctrine that contaminates and eats away like a cancer. One silly analogy that seemed to help our young children grasp the fact that a small amount of false doctrine mixed with truth pollutes purity was what we jokingly referred to as "Dookie in the Brownie." The question that begged an answer was, "Would you eat this brownie if I told you that there was the slightest amount of waste matter in it?" So when they asked to interact with compromised media that would expose their minds to anything we believed was not true, honorable, just, pure, lovely, commendable, excellent, or worthy of praise (Phil. 4:8), we would ask, "Is there dookie in the brownie?" Quite a ridiculous and graphic word picture, but our children definitely got the point! Recently, our daughter discovered that this little timeless treasure is not without a scriptural basis. Ecclesiastes 10:1 says, "Dead flies make the perfumer's ointment give off a stench, so a little folly outweighs wisdom and honor." There are many things that the enemy makes readily available for our children that seemingly look safe to devour. But if truth is mixed with a little bit of untruth—beware! False doctrine is subtle.

One practical suggestion when guarding against the unauthorized entry of unwanted influence is for families to interact together with their books, movies, and games. Use these pastimes as discussion starters to process messages and identify falsehoods. Also, listen to the same music together. Expose your family to strong, God-honoring artists with a variety of genres when your children are young. They are more likely to develop an appetite for healthy music as they are immersed with positive lyrics without compromise. Keep a watchful eye and stay alert to the schemes of the enemy. Scripture warns us, "Be sober-minded; be watchful. Your adversary the devil prowls around like a roaring lion, seeking someone to devour" (I Peter 5:8).

In our efforts to understand the schemes of our adversary, we must be vigilant in clarifying the lines of authority. Guard against power struggles with your children. Conflict quickly rises when we hand over the reins of control too soon. They don't have to be taught how to manipulate. Remember that we all are born like a crooked stick—with a sin nature! This damaging attitude is definitely a respect issue and isn't just a problem with children. Dr. James Dobson has wisely stated,

We must not transfer power too early, even if our children take us daily to the battlefield. Mothers who make that mistake are some of the most frustrated people on the face of the earth. On the other hand, we must not retain parental power too long, either. Control will be torn from our grasp if we refuse to surrender it voluntarily. The granting of self-determination should be matched stride for stride with the arrival of maturity, culminating with complete release during early adulthood.[1]

As a second grade teacher, I recognize this as one of the most dominant areas of struggle in parenting. We must remember from the previous chapter that only when our arrow-children are shaped with the truth will those crooked arrows have any hope of straightness and strength for God's purposes!

Avoid Vulnerability

Our opponent comes in all forms. This next stealer of joy may not be as obvious, but don't discredit the damage it can do to your children. We also must guard against materialism and self-awareness which often lead to a sense of entitlement, covetousness, or envy. We must not allow the line between wants and needs to get blurred. Our flesh has an insatiable desire for more, and we never seem to be satisfied with what we have or how we look. I am speaking to myself here, and I don't think that I am alone in my struggle in this area. The mirror of comparison is always readily available and calling for me to stare into it. It lies every time, and its message is always the same: "If you only had . . . you would be happy." My heart of gratitude and contentment is immediately stolen. I must guard my own heart and the hearts of my children from this enemy by embracing and modeling a thankful, giving, and content heart—one that rejoices and shows appreciation and satisfaction in God's provision. We must remember and speak often to our children of His perfect supply of all good gifts! Our greatest gift? Salvation. Isn't that enough?

The underhanded tactics of the enemy can sneak past our radar in so many areas. This chapter only mentions a few that we've had to deal with, but it would not be complete without mentioning one other area of vulnerability. As a father, Victor always raised the bar high when it came to modesty. Because he was the gatekeeper, so to speak, he was careful to seek God for wisdom and lead his family to not make any provision for the flesh. "But put on the Lord Jesus Christ, and make no provision for the flesh, to gratify its desires" (Rom. 13:14). We cannot feed our self-aware appetites! The implied word of command in this chapter is to watch. Check all motivation for actions and attitudes for modesty at the door. We inwardly dress ourselves in light and righteousness as we put on Christ, and outwardly we want to reflect this same beauty as we walk as children of the light. I love how God uses vivid analogies to illustrate this vital truth. Proverbs 11:22 paints this picture: "Like a gold ring in a pig's snout is a beautiful woman without discretion."

We adorn ourselves so that eyes of others are not drawn to us but to the Giver of all things beautiful, Jesus Christ. This truth is what powered Victor's high standards when it came to the subject of modest clothing for our family. His famous phrase to his girls was, "Keep your body a mystery." At times he even went clothes shopping with them which was done not out of duty, but delight! This topic was mentioned in a recent conversation with our youngest married daughter. She was telling me about how her new husband seemed to be very aware of modesty in her clothing choices. She remarked, "At first I thought, oh man, he sounds just like daddy. I can remember thinking when I was a teenager that I hated it, but secretly I loved it!" So, secretly she treasured that her daddy protected and provided for her purity. Wow. What a great encouragement to all fathers!

Conclusion

In raising a family, the Holy Spirit gives us a clear view of truth during personal daily study through Scripture. Our faith in Him must be steadfast, and knowledge of truth must be ongoing. We must believe that the Bible is true and right about everything in order to recognize lies. We cannot lead and pass on what we ourselves do not possess. The level of obedience to truth that we expect our children to employ will only rise to the level to which we ourselves apply a Scripture permeated filter. This filter of truth should be the plumb line from which everything is measured. He gifts us with discernment and wisdom when we seek His face through the reading of His Word and through prayer. We must be obedient to the knowledge we receive and then trust Him for the results. Be encouraged once again with this truth as you place your confidence in His power: "Unless the LORD builds the house, those who build it labor in vain. Unless the LORD watches over the city, the watchman stays awake in vain" (Ps. 127:1).

ACTION POINTS

1. Write one or two sentences from this chapter that help summarize what you've learned.

   _____

   _____

   _____

   _____

   _____

2. Identify some factors in your family that rob you of quality time together.

   _____

   _____

   _____

   _____

   _____

3. Discuss this statement: Our cell phone obsession may be undermining our lives.

   _____

   _____

   _____

   _____

   _____

4. Why is it difficult for people to completely escape from technology and activity to spend time seeking truth from God's word?

_____

_____

_____

_____

How can you limit the use of technology in your home?

_____

_____

_____

_____

5. How would you define modesty?

_____

_____

_____

_____

What are some ways to communicate its importance?

_____

_____

_____

_____

6. What is one specific way you can guard the hearts and minds of yourself and your children and thwart the enemy's schemes to infiltrate your home?

_____

_____

_____

_____

7
DIRECTING THEIR PATH

I grew up as the oldest of three boys with a Master Sergeant military dad who excelled at giving commands and orders that were clear and usually not up for debate. Because of the definite lines of authority established by birth order, I was the responsible brother who should have known better.

Of course, with three boys about one year apart, fierce, competitive play was the norm. On one occasion our game was a contest of target practice. Walter, my middle brother, and I were the shooters using the adolescent weapon of choice: the Daisy Red Ryder BB gun. Unfortunately, Sammy, our youngest brother, was the target. Rummaging through our garage we found some of dad's old fatigues including a heavy jacket, helmet, boots, etc. The rules were simple. Sammy would run around our three-quarters of an acre backyard in Miami while we shot at him. Fun for us—scary for him. Of course the real challenge, and what made this game so much fun, was trying to hit a moving target. We usually knew when we succeeded due to the distinctive prepubescent yelp that came from Sammy.

Parenting is like hitting a moving target. There must be a continuous recalibration of our parenting techniques which must also take into account a myriad of other moving components: aging parents, a rapidly changing culture, or different personalities, just to name a few. It would be a deadly mistake of profound proportions to utilize the same parenting practices through every developmental stage of our children. At the risk of overstating the obvious, I wouldn't use the same parenting practices on my 16-year-old son that I used when he was five, which is precisely why we need a fixed-point perspective to guide our ever-changing parenting practices.

Our youngest daughter, Julianna, shares an account of how using a fixed-point perspective guided her safely home while lost alone in downtown Almaty, Kazakhstan when she was 16. We'll let her tell her story.

June 8, 2008

I waited at the bus stop alone, hearing the nonsensical language of Russian spoken all around me. Bus 96 came to a screeching stop. Pushing and shoving I squeezed my tiny body onto the bus. I was told to get off when the bus had completed its route. I could walk off the bus, without having to converse in Russian, and walk straight to the house at which I was staying in Almaty, Kazakhstan. I had been in Almaty, the old capital city of Kazakhstan, for two weeks. Having been a capital city at one point, there were many neighborhoods, communities, buildings, and shops in Almaty. But because of the former government being Communist, all shops and houses looked very similar to each other: uniform and equal. Sitting on the bus, I placed my ear buds in my ears, listened to my American music, and attempted to silence the foreign language and culture that were too loud for me to handle. I had just come from three hours of Russian language learning and felt overwhelmed. I had wanted to dive into the lifestyle, but I felt as if I had dove into the ocean rather than an eight-foot pool. I had gone too deep, and the pressure was too much. Singles, families, elderly: everyone had slowly been exiting the bus.

Now it was just the bus driver, the money collector, and me on the bus. The money collector came up to where I was sitting. I took out my ear buds, removing my sense of comfort, and she asked me, rather harshly, something in Russian. Or it may have even been Kazakh. Whatever she had said to me, I had not a clue. Sensing that she possibly wanted me off the bus, I gathered my things, handed her my 50 Tenge and dashed off the bus. However, when I got off of the bus, I was not where I was supposed to be. I just started walking, with no real direction in mind, simply looking around for any signs of familiarity. Here I was, an American girl, dressed in bright colors, listening to her iPod, rather than her phone blasting aloud for all to hear like every other local Kazakh teenager, looking obviously lost. As I was trying to find my way back to the house, I felt as if I were walking in circles, passing the same men at their construction sites. Buildings and houses started to look familiar, but I did not know if I recognized them because I had walked by them multiple times in the past thirty minutes or because this was near where I lived. After two and a half hours of lonely and tiresome roaming the streets of Almaty, I reached home. I found the house by not plainly wandering, but I instead remembered that the day before I had taken pictures on my camera of the walk home from language lessons. As I was looking through my pictures, I saw this tall, monstrous, brown, snowcapped mountain. I glanced up, spotted that mountain, and jogged in its direction, too excited to simply walk. The missionary I was staying with was in tears by the time I reached the house. The mountain in my picture had led me back home! But it was because I had a focal point and direction that I was able to make it to the house. If not, I would have been wandering for hours more.

Julianna's steps were guided by her focus on a fixed-point perspective: the snow covered Tien Shan mountain range that loomed large as the backdrop to the house where she was staying.

Likewise, in parenting, our principles and practices, though applied in a continuously changing environment, must be secured and sustained by the timeless, immutable Word of God. There will always be the temptation to rely on the familiar: what my parents did or what other parents are doing. We need to resist the occasional glance at the constantly changing world's parenting system and instead fix our gaze continually on Jesus "who is the same yesterday and today and forever" (Heb. 13:8). Proverbs 4:25-27 says, "Let your eyes look directly forward, and your gaze be straight before you. Ponder the path of your feet; then all your ways will be sure. Do not swerve to the right or to the left; turn your foot away from evil."

So what does it look like to practically direct our children's paths with a fixed-point perspective? Two verses come to mind that will provide a firm footing and a true North setting to guide our parenting principles and practices:

> Go therefore and make disciples of all nations, baptizing them in the name of the Father and of the Son and of the Holy Spirit, teaching them to observe all that I have commanded you. And behold, I am with you always, to the end of the age (Matt. 28:19–20).

> Hear, O Israel: The LORD our God, the LORD is one. You shall love the LORD your God with all your heart and with all your soul and with all your might. And these words that I command you today shall be on your heart. You shall teach them diligently to your children, and shall talk of them when you sit in your house, and when you walk by the way, and when you lie down, and when you rise. You shall bind them as a sign on your hand, and they shall be as frontlets between your eyes. You shall write them on the doorposts of your house and on your gates (Deut. 6:4-9).

Our aim is active, intentional movement toward heart transformation, not merely behavior modification. We have absolutely no power to fundamentally change our children's hearts with rules and rewards. The law cannot change what only God's grace can achieve. This profound truth frees us from the burden of forcing us to produce change in our children. It can only encourage us, as warrior parents, to recognize that our greatest need is to know and love our King and all that He loves. Scripture gives us the knowledge, and the Holy Spirit will enable and provide every resource we need, like wisdom, discernment, and understanding, to guide our children in the moments of opportunity He gives us. This is a progression and takes time, diligence, and patience. This movement begins with our example to live in utter dependence on God and mirror the gospel message of Romans 15 by bearing with one another, building each other up, and blessing one another. 1 Corinthians 11:1 should be our echo, "Be imitators of me, as I am of Christ." We have been chosen and called by God to guide, instruct, and teach. Everything we teach our children is legitimized inside the home because our children observe, examine, and evaluate everything we say and do. A life that matters is disciples making disciples. The parent is the primary discipler.

There is an *as you go* component in parenting that is clearly stated in both of these verses. It is a means of modeling and transferring with intentionality your love relationship with God to your spouse and children. It is a life that is absorbed with the light of Jesus Christ and reflects that same gospel of kindness, forgiveness, and faithfulness in our everyday life. This is worship.

As you go,

Engage Affections

My love relationship with God should be obvious to all, but especially to my children. I am the same person at church, at home, and at the ballfield. If my child is asked, "What is a distinguishing mark of your dad?" his consistent first response should be, "He loves God." As stated earlier, there should be clarity in the rankings of my affections: God first, spouse second, and children third. These priorities shield me from child-worship and also shield my children from thinking that they are the center of the universe. This cultivates gratitude when they realize as they approach adulthood that the world does not rotate around them.

I recall an incident with one of our adolescent children when her behavior was reflecting a self-centered attitude. My response at that time was immortalized by all three of our children. This was, however, not my intent. But as a grandparent looking back, I'm glad we can still laugh together about it. I remember sitting our child down and holding up my close-fisted right hand and saying, "This is you," and then raising my close-fisted left hand and saying, "This is the world." I then made a motion with my left hand revolving around my right hand being accompanied by these now famous words, "The world does not revolve around you!" Not sure if it was the clichéd nature of this illustration, or my bulging eyes that made this an oft-repeated Flores family moment. Nonetheless, it stuck, and a necessary point was made.

The establishment of ranked affections in my family relationships also promotes security in the lives of my children. I am to love God as my all-satisfying treasure, which means my King holds my attention and affection above every other allegiance, including my family. The greatest gift to my family is to love Christ and His Word supremely. "But seek first the kingdom of God and his righteousness, and all these things shall be added to you" (Matt. 6:33). In humble dependence on Christ, my lifestyle must reflect His character revealed in every book of the Bible. I am charged by my King to display to my children what He is like.

One way to engage and transfer this affection of God to my children is beginning each day with praise, complimenting Him for who He is. Remembering His strong characteristics of power and authority guards our hearts and minds from lies and intimidation from the enemy. I remember that when my wife dropped off our oldest daughter in high school, they would each write the same attribute of God on their hand to help encourage internal God-confidence instead of self-confidence. Of course, this same action can be done in many other creative ways. We also like to use the ABC's to verbalize praise, using each letter of the alphabet to name a unique, exclusive, everlasting attribute of our worthy Savior. To leave a legacy of praise, our children must be immersed in an environment of praise. In other words, my kid's affections for God are stirred up to move beyond just *knowing* to be loving, to move beyond just *thinking* about God, to move beyond just a *feeling* for God. This can only happen when it is modeled in dad and mom. That's leaving a legacy of praise.

Build Knowledge of God's Word

> My son, keep my words and treasure up my command-ments with you; keep my commandments and live; keep my teaching as the apple of your eye; bind them on your fingers; write them on the tablet of your heart (Prov. 7:1-3).

> "We should endeavor by all means possible to make the word of God familiar to us, that we may have it ready to us upon all occasions, for our restraint from sin and our direction and excitement to our duty. It must be as that which is graven on the palms of our hands, always before our eyes."[1]

It should be obvious to others that we regularly hear from God, that we truly treasure the timeless truths of God's Word. We cannot teach that which we do not know. We *cannot make* our children learn or know (only God can do this), but we *must make* ourselves teach as we go, by making the gospel attractive to our children through our example!

Several years ago, our family sold our house of fourteen years to move next door to our good friends who also happen to be our oldest daughter's in-laws. We saw visions of great holiday moments sharing the grandchildren! However, it was a move that exacted a massive emotional toll on me. As we were cleaning and packing, there was a constant stream of memory-making moments with my children replaying themselves in my head. Many of those were punctuated with countless childhood firsts. I was having a hard time letting go. The difficulty of this process hit its peak when it came time to paint the walls in our children's rooms. Over the course of many years our children had taken the time, with great artistic flare, to meticulously grace their walls with favorite scripture passages. Needless to say, applying paint on those walls held a challenge all its own.

At the risk of appearing to take undue credit, I believe it is safe to say that our children's choice of blanketing themselves with walls full of scripture passages was a direct result of growing up in a home where the use of and love for God's Word was preeminent. This posture would be in keeping with the scripture-loving admonition we find in Deuteronomy 6:8-9: "You shall bind them as a sign on your hand, and they shall be as frontlets between your eyes. You shall write them on the doorposts of your house and on your gates."

As we mentioned previously, a major point in parenting is to pass on to the next generation an unwavering, all-encompassing, passionate, sell-everything, stop-at-nothing love for God. That kind of God-love manifests an undeniable gravitational pull our children will find difficult to resist. What we delight in is what they will desire.

I'm not sure if I could have made this statement ten years ago: the older I get, the more I like routine and sameness! Yet, I'm learning to enjoy owning this geriatric-defining way of life. One of my favorite, most dearly held routines is my early morning meeting with the Lord. This appointment is characterized by time, location, and supplies—always the same. Recently our youngest married daughter, Julianna, was visiting for an overnight stay. The following morning, with java in hand, she interrupted my morning routine with the words, "I knew I would find you here!" Until she reads this sentence in this book, she'll never know how much that simple acknowledgement blessed my heart. I have come to realize that I should stare at

Jesus so that when my children stare at me, they see me staring at Jesus.

Many amazing materials are available to help children hear and apply God's Word in a digestible format (see Recommended Reading). Take time, even if it's once a week, to read, discuss, and memorize scripture together as a family. Maybe you could even have one verse a month that you all work on together. Get suggestions of verses from everyone in the family. Another practical idea to have Scripture always before our eyes would be to frame verses around the house.

My wife often tells of her growing up experience in a family of eight reading *The Daily Bread* devotional and reciting Ephesians 4:32 every night after dinner. She knows that verse well!

As you go,

Transmit Truths

So that they should set their hope in God and not forget the works of God, but keep his commandments (Ps. 78:7).

You shall teach them diligently to your children, and shall talk of them when you sit in your house, and when you walk by the way, and when you lie down, and when you rise (Deut. 6:7).

This truth we are transmitting is a life of confidence in God. We remember and set our hope in Him alone. These passages from Psalms and Deuteronomy pretty much nail it. What is the dominant topic of conversation in your home? Who is setting the agenda? Fathers, we have been given the responsibility as captain of the ship! It is our job to set the course for intentional, scheduled God-talk and family devotionals, but also to gently influence and guide casual conversation. The internal sufficiency that we find in Christ will externally be seen and heard through these *as you go* chats. You'll remember from the "Fashioning the Arrows" portion of this book, we were reminded to *take time to tell them the truth*! This is an absolute essential. There is no other way. Jesus said, "I am the way, and the truth, and the life. No one comes to the Father except through me" (John 14:6). This truth that we treasure will inspire our children to trust, follow, and worship this same King.

However, there is one major pre-requisite: proximity. You must be there. Be there in heart, mind, and body. We take time with what we treasure. Another one of those dad routines that I enjoyed when our children were growing up was my nightly arrival home from work. As a student pastor, Wednesday evening and weekends were typically irregular and occasionally there were those weekday committee meetings. But my wife and I preserved as many Mondays as possible for family night. Each week was assigned to one of our children. They were in charge of the dinner menu, devotional, and activity for the evening. It always concluded with my reading to all three of them by our fireplace that was rarely lit since we lived in Florida! One allegory that our family still vividly remembers reading together was the children's version of the classic book *Hinds Feet on High Places* by Hannah Hurnard. The plot allowed our family to take a journey with a crippled girl who chose to leave her valley and travel with the Shepherd to the High Places. The illustrations gave our children a visual of how her enemies like jealousy, anger, pride, and self-pity whispered lies and how they might have looked if they had human faces. These enemies tried relentlessly to deter her from reaching her destination. The little girl in the story only had to call out the Shepherd's name to make them flee. Now, as adults, they all still remember the powerful truths from this book.

I have sweet memories of our children engaged in their nightly routines. Melanie was usually the first to settle in for the night in her bedroom, the last room down the hall on the right. I made it my practice to make my way to her room first. She had a waterbed that inspired a particularly enjoyable (for me anyway) element of our nightly routine. I would press as hard as I could on the opposite side of the watery mattress which caused a violent wave action that had her laughing and rolling about the bed. Once the mattress settled, I would plop down beside her to talk about the highs and lows of her day. Melanie enjoyed sharing, and I enjoyed listening. No questions were ever off limits. Sometimes these discussions would last for a while! I can recall nights walking down the hall anticipating our visit together and fighting the temptation to skip one. However, as I now reminisce about these special moments together, I'm so glad I persisted. Our conversations with all three children were never an interruption or a hassle.

On those occasions when I would stray from prioritizing time with our kids over my household duties, one of our kids would find a way to remind me. I'll never forget the day my son, Tyler, who was about 7 years old at the time, asked me to do something with him. I unwisely responded with a phrase I'm certain he heard much too often, "Can't do that right now. Gotta do work in the yard."

His response was riveting and very much a game changer for me as his father. "Dad!" he sighed, "you love the grass more than me!" I'm sure I replied with evidence to the contrary with that father-knows-best tone. But his missile-like words penetrated deeply.

The moments in which I did respond positively became not only great relationship builders, but opportunities for me to influence and guide God-glorifying conversations that would transmit transformational truth!

Another way you can tell of Jesus as you go would be to make moments matter. The family setting is fraught with these truth-telling signposts that always point back to our Warrior King. Shared experiences, whether joyful or unpleasant, are the glue that bonds families together, which is why we made it a point to have yearly family vacations. As a dad and student pastor,

I find myself keenly observant of these moments, not because I am such a spiritual guy, but because so often these familial moments become illustrations for my weekly messages! On my office wall I have posted one of my favorite Flores family moments that our son captured in writing. On November 23, 2007, Tyler wrote in his journal,

THE MOMENTS

The music was just loud enough to be heard and fill the room, but not so loud as to drown out the merry popping of the fire in the hearth. Julianna lay asleep on the couch, content under the warm red and white blanket. Next to me, Patrick bounced little Lydia Grace on his lap, gently telling her how much he loved her and thought she was the most beautiful little girl in the whole world. Dad lay off to my left, apparently asleep but secretly enjoying every moment of his family together in this quiet sanctuary nestled in the Blue Ridge Mountains. Mom was in the kitchen preparing a simple meal that we all were excited for. She was humming along with the faint music.
The fire popped.

Melanie smiled at her husband as she walked by with laundry balanced on her hip. Anyone peering in through the frosted window could have seen the adoration in her eyes as she gazed on her own small family.

And here sit I, pondering the beautiful simplicity of this moment. Yet even as I write, Julianna groggily climbs off of the couch, her hair in disarray, Lydia begins to whine, and Melanie is remembering to finish the laundry. But for a moment I understood the fleeting gift that life is. Christ only gives us one; and in it, the moments like this are few and far between. So, I am choosing to embrace these moments and thank the One from whom these moments come.

Moments like these don't have to be confined to only occurring in a cabin in North Carolina while on vacation. An attitude of making moments matter as you go should be an attitude we employ in our everyday lives at home. Slow down and create God-honoring memories that point our children to the Giver of all good gifts.

One simple technique Esther and I used to foster an attitude of harmony in our home was to refer to ourselves as Team Flores. We were not individuals living under that same roof; we were *Team Flores! One for all, all for one!* We hoped that this mawkishly sentimental phrase would promote unity of mission in our sanctuary. You and your children could even produce your own timeless motto or family mission statement that uniquely characterizes your family. It would demonstrate your God-given purpose, vision, and direction, giving evidence of His grace in your lives.

Our home should also be a sanctuary of safety. I recall that when all three of our kids were in their early teens, I found myself especially sensitive to how they perceived their home life. This awareness was no doubt a direct result of my position as a student ministry pastor. It was clear to me that there was a direct correlation between spiritually healthy students and spiritually healthy families where the gospel was not marginal but absolutely central. I knew that our children would face challenges to their faith as teens going to a large public high school. I wanted desperately for them to view our home as a sanctuary of safety, a place of refuge where the gospel would be reflected through grace, mercy, love, forgiveness, acceptance, kindness, affirmation, encouragement, protection, understanding, honor, and laughter. Lots of laughter! The kid's form of joy was fun and play. Their favorite reminiscent stories of childhood usually center on the times when their little bodies, bound in big camp T-shirts, were dragged and swirled around and around on our shiny wood floors, and their screams of stopping were ignored! Our home was filled with exuberance and delight which beautifully reflected the fullness of God's pleasure in His children. We trusted that this would counterbalance the onslaught of anti-God influence they would receive on a regular basis. This safe place of refuge of course did not mean tacit approval of all behavior. There were clear guidelines, expectations, and consequences, but they knew that there would never be any action or mistake that would diminish God's or our unconditional love. If our children do walk away from this light, we must always remember and trust that God hears, sees, and cares. He will patiently and ceaselessly pursue His children.

I remember how God taught one of our kids this important message. One day I received a call from our daughter's high school teacher to let us know she had been caught cheating on a test. When I confronted her about this, what distinctly was put on my heart was to use this incident to remind her that God loved her so much that He allowed her to get caught so that cheating would not become the norm. I wanted to impress upon her that we loved her unconditionally just as God loved her unconditionally. In other words, we always wanted to be sure our children knew that a light was left on and the doorway to home was always open!

I believe the most prolific means of transmitting truth with the greatest likelihood of lifelong change in our children is participation in an extended or short-term mission journey. I say this based on the experience of almost thirty years of hosting and leading students and adults (on many occasions with parents and students participating together) and seeing the lasting effects of these experiences. However, without a doubt the most compelling evidence for this assertion is the awakening of undeterred devotion to Jesus I witnessed in my own children while serving on missions journeys.

There will always be a need and a place for highly orchestrated, truth-transmitting events like family devotions and church programs. However, the non-scripted, as-you-go, tell-of-Him moments, such as mission journeys, will transform your child's image to match the perfect image of his or her Creator. Paul writes that we are to "put on the new self, which is being renewed in knowledge after the image of its creator" (Col. 3:10). The transformative experience of a mission journey can be likened to the transformative experience of switching to a 1080 high definition color television after years of watching a black and white set!

As I just stated, there are, of course, other contributing factors which can be employed to transmit truth in our families. The point I am making is that since we are speaking about transmitting truth as you go, sharing and serving together is an environment replete with authentic, truth-transmitting moments! The power of example, especially the life example modeled by a parent, cannot be overstated.

As you go,

Prioritize Prayer

In his message entitled "The Weapon Serves the Wielding Power," John Piper used a great word picture for prayer. He explains,

> God has given us prayer not as an intercom for increased convenience in our secluded cottages, but as a wartime walkie-talkie connecting the general's headquarters with the transportation line and the field hospital and the front line artillery. Prayer is not a bell to call the servants to satisfy some desire we happen to feel, it is a battlefield transmitter for staying in touch with the general . . .The reason the Father gives the disciples the gift of prayer is because Jesus has given them a mission."[2]

We are encouraged in 1 Chronicles 16:11 to "seek the LORD and his strength; seek his presence continually." We have access to God! This mission to advance the gospel through our lives and the sending out of our children can be accomplished through prayer. It would seem to me that as followers of Christ we know intuitively that we need to pray. Praying is needed; praying is good. I would even go as far as to say that there is no greater weapon in the believer's arsenal with as much fire power as God-dependent praying. Yet, experience would tell me it is our least-used weapon. There could be a variety of reasons for this. You fill in the blanks. My appeal to you at this point is to remind you that, as the primary discipler of your children, prioritizing prayer in parenting is a non-negotiable. Going back to our premise: we are in a battle! Apart from this recognition we are susceptible to the schemes of the enemy, and there will be collateral damage. Much is at stake: the advancement of the gospel and the souls of our sons and daughters!

Jesus has paved the way so that we can have complete and unhindered access to our heavenly Father who loves us. Years ago, I had the distinct privilege of visiting the White House with some members of our church staff. This was no ordinary visit. Our visit was hosted by the head of White House security. I vividly remember walking into areas off limits to the public. There were rooms and offices that would have been impossible for me to enter alone. But because of who I was with, and his position, no security personnel stopped me. His presence and position of authority were all the credentials I needed! I remember feeling pretty good about life at the time!

As a child of the King of Kings and Lord of Lords, I have complete access to the throne room of the King of the ages. No special name badges, no ID verifications, no calling ahead to schedule an appointment. Just 24/7, undaunted access. We are reminded in Scripture,

> Since then we have a great high priest who has passed through the heavens, Jesus, the Son of God, let us hold fast our confession. For we do not have a high priest who is unable to sympathize with our weaknesses, but one who

in every respect has been tempted as we are, yet without sin. Let us then with confidence draw near to the throne of grace, that we may receive mercy and find grace to help in time of need (Heb. 4:14-16).

For there is one God, and there is one mediator between God and men, the man Christ Jesus, who gave himself as a ransom for all, which is the testimony given at the proper time (1 Tim. 2:5-6).

Don't miss this! God, creator, sustainer, and consummator, loves you and delights to hear from you, His child, because of Jesus. This realization of a Father-love is my motivation and mode of praying that I am wholly and daily dependent on. My default mental state should begin with the phrase *Dear God*.

So, what does it look like for the warrior-parent to prioritize prayer as you go? Since we believe that God is always with us and that Jesus Christ is our mediator, we should be stopping to fellowship with Him always and about everything. No matter what might be going on in our busy schedules, anytime is worth talking with God by acknowledging His presence and provision, then offering our sacrifices of praise and thanksgiving.

Moreover, we need to pray in partnership with our children as well as in private. My prayer journal assists me each morning as I pray and remember others daily with a weekly schedule of specific names. Our children must be taught this important privilege of intercession in order to cultivate an others-aware attitude. When we pray for each other, God teaches us compassion, stirs our faith, and blesses us with confidence in His character.

At the age of 17, Melanie, our oldest daughter, left for a summer mission adventure in Kazakhstan. This trip was in 2002, one year after the World Trade Centers were attacked. The military were swarming central Asia. Julianna, her sister, writes,

I was 11 years old when my sister left for Kazakhstan, and I started to worry that Melanie would be hurt or unsafe in some way. The way that the LORD really unveiled His obvious omnipresence was in my prayer life. Psalm 3:3-4 says, "But you, O LORD, are a shield about me, my glory, and the lifter of my head. I cried aloud to the LORD, and he answered me from his holy hill." This verse applied to both Melanie and me. She was on the complete opposite side of the world, and yet God was with her to be her shield and her protector, just as He was for me. We both cried aloud and He answered us. Psalm 61:1-2 says, "Hear my cry, O God, listen to my prayer; from the end of the earth I call to you when my heart is faint. Lead me to the rock that is higher than I, for you have been my refuge, a strong tower against the enemy." God was present with us and heard and listened to our call to Him! The God who sees! And that is why our God is so worthy to be praised! The more you recognize Him and see His heart, the more you want to glorify and magnify Him in your life! He deserves our declaration of dependence!

Yes! God daily deserves our declaration of dependence, which is a prerequisite to faith-filled praying morning, noon, and night. We must free ourselves of simply praying for our children to have a good day, but for strength, diligence, and perseverance to know and love Him with all their heart, soul, mind, and strength.

Also, following the example of Christ's intercessory prayer in John 17, we must pray for each other for the sake of the gospel going forth, for unity, for purity, and for joy! Praying scripture reveals God's will and is that powerful weapon Paul spoke about in Ephesians 6 as we fight in this daily battle against the enemy of deceit and unbelief in our lives.

Esther's dad has always been such a role model for us in this area of prayer. I became a recipient of his daily petitions to the Father the day I walked into his house to date his daughter. I knew that he loved God with all his heart and talked with Him unceasingly. I offer my gratitude to this great and humble man for his faithful service preaching the gospel for more than 50 years. He viewed prayer as a delight, a privilege, and a responsibility. In regard to his view on praise and thanksgiving, Esther has shared the story of an early childhood conversation with her dad to many people. She recalls,

> One day I came into my daddy's office with a burdensome question. I wanted to know how to get bad thoughts out of my head. He responded to my question with another question. "Well, sweetheart, how would you get a sharp knife out of a toddler's hand?" I confidently answered with statements like, "Offer him a toy or a cookie?" None of my answers seemed to adequately solve the problem of the toddler still having the harmful object in his hand. Sufficiently frustrated, I raised my tiny voice and responded, "Just tell me!" He patiently replied, "No, you hold out two cookies. One for each hand. Then the child will drop the knife." Daddy went on to explain this analogy by encouraging me that every time I have a bad thought, it's like that harmful knife. The two cookies are a picture of praise and thanksgiving. So when I want to rid myself of harmful thoughts that may lead to sin, I must replace them with praise, giving a compliment to God for who He is, and thanksgiving for what He has done. I have to admit, it works every time!

I overheard my wife's conversation the other day as she was talking to Julianna. After attentive listening, she advised, "Well, Jules, you know what to do! Go into your closet, shut the door, and eat two cookies!" Praise and thanksgiving are perfect nourishment for the soul!

This admonishment to prioritize prayer as you go would not be complete without mentioning the small chalkboard that our daughter Melanie has on her kitchen counter. At the top is printed, "Today, I am thankful for." Her little family tries to write something new every week. It reminds me of the verse in Psalm 78:

> "We will not hide them from their children, but tell to the coming generation the glorious deeds of the LORD, and his might, and the wonders that he has done" (Ps. 78:4). This expression of thanksgiving keeps us mindful of God's rich abundance lavished on us!

As you go,

Live Generously

When I think of Christmas, among the many happy memories is busting out the classic movie *It's a Wonderful Life* and watching it together as a family. This tradition is always on the top of our list, not just because it is a great movie, but the title actually captures our family's Christmas attitude. Esther is one of those moms who is very good at establishing and maintaining family traditions, even on those days when there may have been those collective moans and groans from the kids (of course never from me). Nevertheless, she would press on even when the TV still had the AFC/NFC playoff game going on in the background with the sound off, of course. And sometimes when the forced memory making moments were over, through tears of joy and heartfelt gratitude, we all would express appreciation to her faithfulness to maintain these vestiges of yuletide cheer. Christmas was always a happy time, a reminder of what a wonderful life it is.

Until that one Christmas. As our children were opening presents, there was an obvious growing deficit in the thankfulness and appreciation category. Needless to say, this was pretty discouraging and somewhat unusual to us. While Esther and I were cleaning up after all the commotion of gift opening was over, we both agreed that the ungrateful attitudes were unacceptable, so we cooked up a plan. We contacted a local ministry that provided gifts for underprivileged children. We arranged to have all three of our kids come on the day they would be organizing and distributing gifts. What began as a learning opportunity for our children became a game-changer in our parenting attitude and arsenal. First of all, our children thoroughly enjoyed this experience. Second, we participated together as a family in serving others, deepening and extending family bonds. Third, the hearts of our kids were positively affected in the area of appreciation for all of God's provisions. This was huge and something I vowed to file away as a tremendous family ministry necessity: living generously by serving the LORD with gladness (Ps. 100:2)!

Serving is a vital component of discipleship. This new element of prioritizing the preciousness of others began to entrench itself in our family's DNA. We tried to be vigilant also to set examples of honored, active service through our faithful attendance and cheerful giving to that which He loves, our church, the bride of Christ. It is essential that our children be exposed to this level of commitment, the value of community, and the body working together for the cause and fame of the King.

The transforming power of the gospel becomes evident when our children make generous decisions that have been inwardly motivated from a love for God, as opposed to outward parental pressure or expectations. We witnessed this with our youngest daughter. At the age of 16, Julianna experienced the smile of God when she anonymously gave the first 500 dollars she earned at her new job to a friend that needed money for the student mission trip to Brazil. I have to admit that when I found out about this sacrifice, I was a little dismayed knowing she had a long way to go to meet her own financial obligation for a trip to Kazakhstan. A week or two later, God taught me a lesson on trust and encouraged her active obedience when a church member handed her a check for 500 dollars, the exact amount she had given away! This was a reminder to me that God honors us when we live generously.

We should always be looking for ways to pour our lives into others by faithfully giving and serving God side-by-side with our family, as we go.

A parenting axiom that I've grown accustomed to using is that what we as parents do in moderation, our kids will do to an extreme. I find this true for several reasons. But primarily I believe this is the result because children, especially teens by nature, live on the edge on extreme. I usually use this in the context of negative behavior; however, I believe this truth also holds true positively, and the example I would offer is in serving and missions. If your child perceives that serving others is important to his parents, especially dad, they will tend to do the same, but bigger and better! Parents, let your kids see you serving others.

My greatest joy has been witnessing the awakening of an attitude of service in all three of our children that was fueled by each participating in extended mission trips and in joining me in our short-term student mission trips to Brazil each year. These types of trips are not only profitable in transmitting truths (as mentioned earlier) but when children become an eye-witness to their parents serving others, it makes an unforgettable impact on them spiritually. When we live a life of service as a response to God's sacrificial love and provision, we recognize our purpose for being alive, which is to join our King in His mission: to push back the darkness by bringing light and life to all nations!

This exhortation to live a generous life of service as we direct our arrows toward the heart of God would not be complete without bringing my hero named Bert Elliot into the center ring. Did you know that Jim Elliot had a brother? Bert is the older, not-so-famous one. He referred to Jim as "a great meteor streaking through the sky." Bert faithfully ministered alongside his wife in Peru for 62 years, planting and establishing 150 congregations. Bert joined his brother Jim to enjoy his reward in heaven on February 17, 2012.

Trevin Wax, a contributor to thegospelcoalition.org, wrote an article entitled "Jim Elliot's Brother, Bert: The Hero You Don't Know." He states,

> Last month, I had a conversation with Michael Kelly about his book *Boring: Finding an Extraordinary God in an Ordinary Life*. Michael tells the story of Bert Elliot, brother to missionary Jim, as an example of what faithfulness over a lifetime looks like. For those of us who are not "meteors streaking across the sky," it serves as a reminder of how we can be a steady light for the gospel no matter where God has placed us. . .
>
> In the kingdom of God, there is a great need for streaking meteors, but most of us won't be that. We will instead be faint stars—husbands and fathers, wives and mothers. We will be accountants and teachers, business people, and students. We will go through life, day after day, doing very much the same thing tomorrow that we did today.
>
> The important thing for us to remember is that we are needed. There is a great need for people willing to chase the little donkeys of life, not because it's exciting but because they believe in the constant presence and purpose of God. There is a great need for people willing to stand in the midst of the boring, convinced that there is no such thing as ordinary when you follow an extraordinary God.
>
> Rise and stand. Then tomorrow, do it again.[3]

Bert, (unlike his brother Jim) never had a movie made about him, and there are no framed quotes made by him. Yet, Bert faithfully lived out the calling God placed on his life, and because of his obedience to "rise and do it again" each day, the landscape of heaven will be forever changed. Bert lived his life to reflect the example of Jesus: "For even the Son of Man came not to be served but to serve, and to give his life as a ransom for many" (Mark 10:45).

Conclusion

This *as you go* parent discipleship model is an intentional sharing, showing, and teaching of the light and love of Jesus that mirrors an attractive gospel to our children as we direct their path. This lifestyle of worship is one that is captivated by the beauty of God's grace and responds to our spouse and children with the same gospel of kindness, forgiveness, and faithfulness in our everyday life. Remember, when our children stare at us, they should see us staring at Jesus!

ACTION POINTS

1. Write one or two sentences from this chapter that help summarize what you've learned.

   _____

   _____

   _____

   _____

   _____

2. What are some ways your family can delight in the King and His gospel every day?

   _____

   _____

   _____

   _____

   _____

3. In your family's journey, what role does Scripture memory play?

   _____

   _____

   _____

   _____

What can you begin to do to keep it always before their eyes?

_____

_____

_____

_____

4. What is the dominant topic of conversation in your home?

_____

_____

_____

_____

Who sets the agenda?

_____

_____

_____

_____

5. Share some ways your family maximizes moments and conversation to build deeper relationships.

_____

_____

_____

_____

6. What is your typical response when your children mess up?

    _____

    _____

    _____

    _____

    How can you have a gospel-centric answer?

    _____

    _____

    _____

    _____

7. What prayer do you pray privately for your family?

    _____

    _____

    _____

    _____

    Have you ever shared it with them?

    _____

    _____

    _____

    _____

8. CHALLENGE: Develop a mission statement or motto to demonstrate your God-given purpose, vision, and direction for your family.

_____

_____

_____

_____

8

RELEASING WITH INTENTION

If you were asked to name your favorite Bible story, how would you respond? Many of you might say that "David and Goliath" is your favorite.

Against All Odds

I'd like to camp here with David and Goliath for a moment. While I won't take the time to retell the entire story, I will point out the following. We know from 1 Samuel 17 that David, because of his age, size, and military experience, was at a tremendous disadvantage in his epic battle against Goliath. To any observer, it was obvious that apart from supernatural intervention David was doomed to sure defeat at the hands of this battle-hardened, expertly-equipped, and highly decorated foe. Yet against all odds, David defeated Goliath. Was it the fact that David was outfitted with all the latest weaponry money could buy or that he was trained at the finest military schools?

No. David had what mattered most: a heart, head, and hand that trusted in Almighty God to do the impossible. David had done his part to wield his slingshot and launch the stone. Upon release of the stone, it was the hand of God that guided it to its foreordained target. David's display of acting in faith, obediently and courageously, brought victory to the entire nation of Israel that day.

Your Secret Weapon Won't Do It

Contrast this victorious display of faithful obedience that trusted in the hand of God with a lesser known story of trusting in the hand of man with disastrous results.

1 Samuel 4:1-11 records the story which is also referenced in Psalm 78. This story takes place many years before David arrives on the scene. Some quick background is needed. To get and appreciate the context of this story, we have to go to I Samuel 3 where we quickly learn that this was a dark time in the history of Israel. Verse one says, "Now the young man Samuel was ministering to the LORD under Eli. And the word of the LORD was rare in those days; there was no frequent vision" (1 Sam. 3:1).

But because of God's grace, verse 3 says that "the lamp of God had not yet gone out" (1 Sam. 3:3). The remainder of Chapter 3 is the account of the Lord calling Samuel to be God's voice during these dark days. One of the first things the Lord tells Samuel is that God is about to pour out judgment on Eli's family "because his sons were blaspheming God, and He did not restrain them" (1 Sam. 3:13).

Shortly after God's call on Samuel's life, we read the account of Israel, the tribe of Ephraim, going into battle with the Philistines. Israel is soundly defeated in this battle. After their defeat, Israel picks up the pieces and prepares to go to battle with the Philistines again. This time they send their secret weapon, the Ark of God. The Israelites reasoned that surely the presence of the Ark would ensure their victory! However, the two guys in charge of the Ark are the disobedient sons of Eli. Israel is defeated, and the two sons of Eli are killed.

Consider what we know about the Ephraimites. They were known and admired for their warrior prowess. They boasted an abundance of valiant men. Not only were they known for their military might, but they also possessed the Ark of God! These advantages made the Ephraimites' defeat all the more staggering and shocking.

So why the unexpected loss for Ephraim? A reading of Psalm 78 reveals the answer:

> The Ephraimites, armed with the bow, turned back on the day of battle. They did not keep God's covenant, but refused to walk according to his law. They forgot his works and the wonders that he had shown them (Ps. 78:9-11).

> Yet they sinned still more against him, rebelling against the Most High in the desert. They tested God in their heart by demanding the food they craved (Ps. 78:17-18).

> Because they did not believe in God and did not trust his saving power (Ps. 78:22)

> But they flattered him with their mouths; they lied to him with their tongues. Their heart was not steadfast toward him; they were not faithful to his covenant (Ps. 78:36-37).

> They did not remember his power or the day when he redeemed them from the foe (Ps. 78:42).

I could go on. There are many, many more verses like these that detail the rebellious and unrepentant acts of Israel.

But back to the comparison of David's victory and Ephraim's loss. Here is the point of my sharing these two contrasting stories.

Outward Accoutrements Only Look Good

Your family can have all the outward accoutrements of position and prestige required to be *that* family. Yet without God as the center of your home, it's unlikely that your child will be launched as an agent of transformation who will join Jesus in pushing back darkness. Remember how well equipped the Ephraimites appeared to be? Yet, without God as their guide, they were doomed to failure. In contrast, David, despite his lack of weaponry and physical prowess, was triumphant because he had what really mattered: a strong heart for God.

Moreover, once David released his weapon, he trusted that God's power would guide, penetrate, and inflict the most damage to the enemy for the victory and glory of the King.

In a similar manner, we as warrior parents must place our love, trust, and allegiance to the King and His mission of light and liberty. We do so in hopes of rescuing those who are spiritually dead and bound in their bondage of darkness. The weapons we have been given to launch straight to the enemy's hosts are our arrow-children, carefully chosen by God and shaped in truth for His eternal purpose. We, the warriors, prayerfully aim and release, but it's the faithful, powerful hand of God alone that directs our arrows for the win and fame of His great name!

The Heart of the Warrior and the Hand of God Matters

This story has brothers and sisters. As Esther and I prayed and thought about writing a book like this, there were several ways in which we both felt God's clear leading. One of them was our familiarity with numerous families who lived out the premise of this manuscript. Since this awareness was high on our list for reasons to proceed in writing, it occurred to us that others might benefit from knowing the stories of some of these families. These letters testify to the worth of a battle fought for the cause of our King.

RELEASING THE ARROW: a warrior's reflection

By Katie

Really, my story of letting go has very little to do with me and everything to do with God. He knew who I was. He knew it would take time for me to get used to the idea of my sweet, blond-haired, blue-eyed daughter going off to Africa. He knew it would take me years to get up to speed. I think that's one reason why He put "orphans in Zambia" on her heart when she was only 14.

She didn't share the Holy Spirit's tug on her heart immediately, but when she did, my first response was, "Uhhhh…no." She was online looking at different organizations that were ministering to orphans in Zambia, wanting to go with them at age 16. I hadn't heard of these organizations, and I didn't know any of the people in charge, so this mama was not even entertaining the idea of sending her baby with them. I didn't say, "Never," just, "Not yet."

After this, she didn't really bring it up too much, but I'd see little paper cut-outs of Africa stuck on her bulletin board with Zambia colored in, or see "Zambia" written here or there. I knew this was more than a passing phase she was going through.

It wasn't until she came home from a night out with friends between her junior and senior years of high school that things started to get real. She was at IKEA with a few people, some of whom she didn't know well at all. They were talking about their last year of high school and what they wanted to do after graduating. Our daughter said something like, "What I really want to do is go to Zambia and work with orphans." One of the girls that she didn't know well gasped and said, "I've been to an orphanage in Zambia, and the family who ran the orphanage is good friends with my family, and they'll be in town soon, and I want to go help orphans in Africa, too, etc." When our daughter came home, she was sooooo excited, and all this information came flowing out all at once. She could hardly catch her breath.

That was the moment that I remember thinking, "God, this is You, isn't it? This is You, making things happen. This is more than a kid's desire to go to Africa." Yes, I'm a little slow. It took years of preparation to get me to a place of surrender. Once I saw that God was in this, and He was putting all of the pieces together, I couldn't help but jump on that train.

Many of my friends had some serious reservations about our daughter going to Africa and thought we were crazy. "She wasn't going with a group? She wasn't with an organization? There wasn't an adult traveling with her?" There was one thing that I knew, though. There was no doubt God's fingerprints were all over this trip. How could I get in the way of something God wanted to do in my daughter's life?

God is such a good God. He continued to put all the pieces together in such a way that there was no doubting who was behind it. He knew this mama needed to see that—this mama who loves her children with a passion, loves to be with them and share in their lives, but also knows that they're God's. They are His.

Our daughter is getting ready to go to college in a few weeks, and I'm more unsettled about that than I was in sending her to Africa. It's weird, but true. Each new situation brings a new challenge. Just when you think you have this "letting go" thing mastered, God says, "Here's a new twist! You still need Me!"

RELEASING THE ARROW: a warrior's reflection
By Lei Ann

I remember when God began to ready my heart for launching my sons to college. I was walking to my car from the Sunday

School class I had just taught and carefully picking my way through the grassy parking lot bordering the railroad track. My grandparents' home once stood on the lot, and my walk was filled with memories. As a child, I played with stray kittens and ate my great grandmother's syrup tea cakes on that same field. Whenever the trains rumbled past, my uncle would scoop me up, put me on his shoulders, and run me down to the tracks to wave to the conductor. Everything about the lot and the church held a memory of my childhood.

But God was now telling me that He wanted my family to leave this place with its treasured memories to serve in a new church.

I didn't like what I heard. Surely I must have misunderstood. My husband and I were married in that church! Both of our sons had been baptized there! What about all our family and friends we'd be leaving behind? I couldn't ask my sons to leave everything and everyone they knew to join a new church.

And that's when God reminded me that in just a few short months, I would be asking my oldest son to do just that. In a few short months, my husband and I would be launching our oldest to college. By asking our family to make the move to a new church home now, God was graciously preparing our son for what lay ahead when he attended a university with a student population larger than our hometown. God was allowing our sons while they still lived at home to learn what it looked and felt like to walk into a new place where they knew no one. He was equipping them to find a new church home by themselves without the security of family.

Moving to a new church home during our son's senior year was not bad timing. It was God's loving provision for two young men in preparation for what lay ahead.

Since that move, God has guided our oldest son through increasingly challenging opportunities. Our son first moved to Gainesville to attend the University of Florida. He later spent a summer working and living by himself in Washington, D.C. He then spent yet another summer living and working by himself in California. At each juncture, our son intentionally sought a new church home, and he felt equipped to find that church home by himself. These church homes have provided him with the Christian community he has needed to face the challenges of a culture that desperately needs Christ. In a time when many of his friends have walked away from God, our son has found churches to help him continue to grow in his faith.

Yes, if I allow myself to dwell on the distance that separates us, I desperately miss my son. I've learned to treasure the texts and phone calls as he walks from the bus stop to campus or from his apartment to the metro. I look forward to his late night phone calls regardless of the hour!

Yes, I miss my son. But I'm blessed to see how God continues to speak through him as he engages his friends, classmates, and coworkers in a God-denying culture.

Our oldest son will soon leave for West Lafayette, Indiana, to attend graduate school at Purdue University. And our youngest son, a recent high school graduate, will soon leave to begin classes at Samford University in Birmingham, Alabama. They'll both walk into new places where they don't know anyone. But our God has lovingly equipped them to meet the challenge.

RELEASING THE ARROW: a warrior's reflection

By Jerry and Beth

Our salvation was made possible because Jesus said to the Father, "Not My will, but Yours be done" (Luke 22:42). His obedience to do what God asked Him to do is what saved us from spending eternity in hell. We live every day with a grateful heart to Christ for saving us, for being obedient to the Father, and we've taught our children from birth to do the same.

Biblical parenting may not be what you think it is! From the time we learned we would have a child, we prayed about their future. We prayed that, above anything else, they would believe God and His Word, that they would love Him, that they would trust Him completely, and that they would follow Him wherever He would lead them, for all of their lives. Like every parent, we want our kids to be healthy, safe, and happy. But we also knew that their holiness was much more important than any of these (Matt. 6:33). We knew that the only way any of us would be truly happy was for us to be in the center of God's perfect will. We've strived for this to be the core and foundation of our parenting.

We knew God gave our children to us for a short while, entrusting us with the responsibility to teach them about Him and His Kingdom. It was our job to prepare them to always follow the Lord's leading as they became adults. We prayed every day (and still do) for their future, that they would always be obedient to God. We even knew that one day He would call us to release them fully to Him, to whatever He wanted them to do. But we didn't fully realize until that day came, that all the years we were preparing our daughter to follow God, He was also preparing US to release her.

All through their childhood, our family has participated in the work of the Church and kept our children involved in the ministries our church provided. In addition to taking them to church, we made it a priority to read the Bible with them at home and to talk about what they learned at church. We made sure they understood that Mom and Dad believe with all our hearts that the Bible is true, God alone is perfect and holy, He loves us unconditionally, and that we trust Him completely. We read about God's power and His miracles starting with creation. We taught them how the heroes of the Bible believed the Lord and obeyed Him wholeheartedly, and that they should do the same for all their lives.

Early in her senior year of high school, our daughter told us God was calling her to serve as a volunteer missionary for 6 to 12 months, right after she graduated high school. Now put yourself in our position; after raising her as we described above, how could we possibly say "no"? How could we say, "That's crazy; it's not safe; it's too expensive. You're too young. You need to get your college education first"? After teaching her for 18 years to love, trust, and obey the God who created her, the God of Noah and the Ark, Moses and the Red Sea, David and Goliath, Daniel and the Lion's Den, Jesus and the Cross of salvation, His love for humanity and His resurrection power…how could we possibly say "no"?!? What hypocrites we would be if we had demanded she do the "normal" American thing after teaching her for her whole life to follow God no matter what! Read the Bible and you will see that God's ways are not "normal" by the world's definition! Of course, our prayers for her (and ourselves) became even more frequent and specific. We asked God to confirm this calling to each of us, and He did!

From her junior year in high school, our daughter was absolutely certain that she should go to culinary school and become a chef. Beginning her senior year, she had already completed 3 years of culinary classes in High School and loved it; so it seemed natural for her to continue that education and training. We researched and visited a few schools, but as parents, we never felt at peace with it although we couldn't pinpoint why. However, our daughter was so sure and enjoyed it so much that we had no good reason to disagree with her plans.

In October of her senior year, our church introduced the GO Term, which is a program for young, single adults to take time off college to serve as a volunteer missionary. We each heard about the GO Term at different times: Mom first, then Dad, then our daughter. As soon as Mom heard about it, she immediately felt the Holy Spirit say, "Our granddaughter may do this!" but she didn't say anything to anyone. When dad heard it, he said to Mom, "What do you think about our granddaughter doing this GO Term?" We agreed that this was very possibly what she should do, but she hadn't heard about it yet! Finally, at our church's annual mission's conference, our daughter was sitting in the worship center with friends when she heard about the GO Term. After the service, she met us in the parking lot with wide eyes and a big smile and said, "The GO Term, that's what I'm supposed to do!"

Initially, our daughter wanted to go to a "hard place," and pursued a term in Israel. Once again, we found ourselves not feeling peace about that decision, yet she was determined to serve out of her comfort zone. All of us continued to pray fervently for God's direction. During our church's Spring Break mission journey for high school students, she returned to Brazil for the third time. While she was there, the Brazilian pastor who the team served with personally invited our daughter to come back to Brazil to serve with his ministry for an extended time. This clearly was God's answer to our prayers for His direction! We and her Youth Pastor believed she should serve in Brazil, and God made that obvious to her as well. In fact, He had been preparing her for two years to do so, during previous Spring Break mission journeys.

Once we were all on the same page, it took much longer than expected for her to get to Brazil. College was postponed another semester because it took 4 months to get an extended visa from the Brazilian government. Our daughter learned patience and to work and serve the Lord in other ways while waiting on His timing.

Finally, eight months after graduating high school, our daughter went to Brazil and served there for ten months. Did we worry she might die? Did we worry she would get really sick? Did we worry she might get hurt? Did we worry she might get kidnapped? Yes, to all of these! But we had more peace about her life during those ten months than we have ever experienced while she lived here with us. This can only be explained by all of us being surrendered to God's will. Yes, she got sick—a lot! Yes, she got hurt a few times. But she didn't die and she didn't get kidnapped! The Lord brought her safely home, more mature, more Christ-like, and even more responsible than ever!

We thank the Lord for giving her such a wonderful opportunity to serve Him and to see the world through His eyes.

RELEASING THE ARROW: a warrior's reflection

By Andy

As a parent you never know just how much freedom to give your children and when exactly to release that freedom. It is our goal to raise up young men and young women to be God-loving and productive citizens here in this life. After all, God has placed that responsibility on all who wish to be known as good, moral, and godly parents. It's called being a Christian parent.

As we all know, children are not ours, but God's. This is easy to say, but hard to do. It's easy to proclaim, but difficult to live out. The Holy Spirit revealed this proclamation to me in a very real and undeniable way one morning while I was piddling in my workshop. The workshop is one of my favorite places to be. It's quiet out there and I spend time with my Lord praying and meditating on His word.

One morning I was enjoying my time with Him and He spoke to me in a very real and powerful way. I was giving Him praise for my life, my family, and for my salvation accredited to me through my faith in Jesus Christ. Then it happened; I was praying for my daughter, Amy, who was in Brazil at the time serving in missions there. I was praying that God would protect my eighteen year old, my only daughter, and my little girl. I was praying "my Amy this" and "my Amy that" and the Holy Spirit stopped me dead in my tracks. "She is not your Amy; she is My servant and you have been a stumbling block to her. Stop it, trust Me more, and become her biggest supporter and encourager.

This revelation was such a shock to me that it took me hours before I could even share it with my sweet wife. That was the day I fully released Amy to the Lord. She will always be my daughter, but, more importantly, my prayer is that she will always be His servant.

RELEASING THE ARROW: a warrior's reflection

By Meg

As a mother, probably the hardest thing to do is give God full control of your child. After investing time in Brazil working with a Christian ministry, my eighteen-year-old daughter decided she wanted to spend the rest of her life there. "I'm Brazilian," she'd tell me. Well, I was okay with her serving the Lord for short-term trips, even months at a time with only Skype or Facebook posts from the group to give me a glimpse of how she was doing. But the rest of her life? "What about when you marry and start a family?" I'd ask. You see, I had a vision, a "dream" of filling the church pew one day with my children, their spouses, and grandchildren week after week, worshipping together, like other families I know. I spent much time in prayer and seeking the Lord and He spoke to my heart in so many ways. He used various pastor's sermons, a book I happened to be reading (*Having a Mary Heart in a Martha World* by Joanna Weaver, *Kisses from Katie* by Katie Davis), even phone calls out of the blue. One of the Brazilian pastor's wives had said to me, "Have you prepared your heart to lose her?" I sensed God was leading my heart to submission, full submission, to whatever He had for our daughter and for us.

And in the end, she did not move to Brazil. God brought her a wonderful, Christian young man and they have recently married. Even so, I may never have my dream of filling the church pew. Because wherever He takes them, near or far, He has the best plans for their lives. I now know that God used our Brazil experience to get me to the place of fully releasing her.

She is not mine. She belongs to Him. And His plans are perfect. "God's ways are higher than mine" (Isa. 55:9).

RELEASING THE ARROW: a warrior's reflection

By Christy

When my daughter was 12, I knew she needed to go to Haiti. I didn't know how or when or any of those important details. I just knew she needed to go! For me, she needed to go and experience a third world country, she needed to appreciate her comfy American life, she needed to see how blessed she was. Unbeknownst to me, God had already had it in His plans for her life, for His reasons, not mine. The following year, my husband and I were taking a parenting class with Victor and Esther, in which they compared the parent-child relationship to that of a warrior-arrow. We need to aim them well and then release. This rocked my world! How could I let my baby girl leave every comfort she knew (and me) to serve in Haiti for a week? I wasn't sure I could, but God had different plans. Every door was opened wide for her. I knew we could not financially do it on our own, but God provided. There was never a stumbling block placed in our way. Now the question changed to, how could I not let her go? The day came for me to shoot my arrow, and man did she fly! It was the hardest day of my life, and I wasn't sure I would make the week without her, but again and again, God showed that His grace is enough. I was texting my mom throughout the day, being comforted by words only my mom could say, and then she wrote this, "Arrow tips are hard and fast. And you have aimed her well!" Wow, thanks for the reminder and encouragement! Our daughter made it through the week loving life and is now counting the days until she can go back to the country where she left her heart. So, what I intended to be a learning experience, God intended to be a heart experience. Once again, God wins!

RELEASING THE ARROW: a warrior's reflection

by Cindy

When I think about whether or not I have released my daughter to serve halfway around the world, I have to admit it is a repeated struggle and decision, not a one-time event. There are so many things on my list of wishes for each of my daughters that are my desires and not necessarily God's or hers. The biggest is that I want her to get married so that she has a partner in serving and is spared from a potentially lonely life. I know she would make a great momma, so I have the hope that she will get to fulfill that desire. If I am perfectly honest, I have to confess that I also want those things for myself. Grandbabies. A reason for her to have to come home. More ties to the United States. As a young lady who is almost six feet tall, being in China on a team of mostly females has limited her opportunities for me to realize all my wishes.

I get to Skype with her almost weekly, a blessing of technology that I now take for granted. When we talk, there is almost always one outstanding impression that I have. She is at peace. She is where she is supposed to be. The gifts that God has bestowed upon her because of her obedience stir up in me a godly jealousy. She has a compassion for her team mates and a wisdom in problem solving that go beyond anything I experience in my daily relationships. Her heart is to see them succeed at teaching and flourish in their walk with the Lord. She has a joy in her purpose and gets to regularly see gospel fruit that doesn't happen to me in my comfortable life. She has adventure and excitement exploring new countries and cultures that can make my life seem very small. She writes music that lifts up the Father with such beauty that it is an act of worship I am not capable of. All of these are from a relationship of intimacy with Christ that she is driven to pursue wholeheartedly, in a way she might not if not for her circumstances.

So my release of her is really a release of ideas that I need to let the Father shape daily. Is she lonely? No more or less than anyone in my home, church, workplace, or neighborhood. Will she have unfulfilled dreams? Yes, don't all of us who thought marriage or children or career would make us whole? Is she happy? Most days, yes. Some days, no. We all are happy or not depending on circumstances that are often out of our control. Is she content? Yes, she is. She has a best friend in Jesus, and her relationship with Him is like no other person I know. I want to be like her when I grow up. God, release me from all my expectations.

RELEASING THE ARROW: a warrior's reflection

The following letter was written by a mother that we haven't met yet, but her response had a profound impact on us when our own children asked to go oversees on extended mission journeys.

By Mrs. Catherine Jane Filson Carmichael

January 16, 1892
My own Precious Child,
He who hath led will lead
All through the wilderness,
He who hath fed will surely feed.
He who hath heard thy cry
Will never close His ear,
He who hath marked thy faintest sigh
Will not forget thy tear.
He loveth always, faileth never,
So rest on Him today—forever.

Yes, dearest Amy, He has lent you to me all these years. He only knows what a strength, comfort, and joy you have been to me. In sorrow He made you my staff and solace, in loneliness my more than child companion, and in gladness my bright and merry-hearted sympathizer. So, darling, when He asks you now to go away from within my reach, can I say nay? No, no, Amy, He is yours—you are His—to take you where He pleases and to use you as He pleases. I can trust you to Him and I do…All day He has helped me, and my heart unfailingly says, "Go ye."[1]

Conclusion

Parenting is faith work. We can't know how it will all turn out. But in obedience, sacrifice, and trust we launch our arrows into a place that we may never see, therefore making it a work of faith in God's powerful, guiding hand.

Psalm 127, from which we have formulated our main treatise, is the place I'd like to return to as we conclude. Verse 1 begins with a strong challenge: "Unless the LORD builds the house, those who build it labor in vain" (Ps. 127:1). The presupposition is clear. Unless the Lord is the designer, builder, and occupier, any attempt to build a home is an audaciously arrogant exercise in futility. Without the Lord as our builder, generation after generation will experience a profound nullifying impact upon eternity. Without the Lord as our builder, our labor will be futile and captives will remain!

Our arrow-children are not ours at all. We must remember that they are an amazing reward from the Lord, given to us from the largeness of His gracious heart. We must be diligent to be good stewards of these divine blessings. God is always at work in and with them. They are His. Therefore, we raise our children not with culture-filled trends but with the Christ-filled truth of God's faith-filled gospel. We then rest with steadfast hearts on His promises and confidence that our good gifts will become useful instruments in the care of a worthy King and released for His service and fame.

Although the premise of *Raise to Release* was birthed from the Psalm 127 reference cited by Jim Elliot, the seed of my familiarity with and admiration for this man actually began with another, more famous quote of his: "He is no fool who gives up what he cannot keep to gain what he cannot lose." Missional parenting to the glory of God is no less than a self-forsaking, God-gaining proposition.

The convicting message that Jim Elliot penned to his parents is still hanging on the wall in our daughter's home:

> Remember how the Psalmist described children? He said that they were as an heritage from the Lord, and that every man should be happy who had his quiver full of them. And what is a quiver full of but arrows? And what are arrows for but to shoot? So, with the strong arms of prayer, draw the bowstring back and let the arrows fly—all of them, straight at the Enemy's hosts.[2]

These words continue to resonate in our hearts with deeper significance as we watch our own three arrow-children become warriors, raising our grandchildren to release.

Our story is still being written, and so is yours. Regardless of your situation, have hope that it's never too late to disciple your children, shaping and directing their hearts to the King and His cause. The devil and his influences for evil are thwarted by gospel-charged children!

In 1868, Mary A. Thompson penned a hymn that beautifully sums up the passion behind this book:

O Zion, Haste
O Zion, haste, thy mission high fulfilling,
To tell to all the world that God is light;
That He who made all nations is not willing
One soul should perish, lost in shades of night.

> *Refrain:*
> Publish glad tidings, tidings of peace;
> Tidings of Jesus, redemption and release.

Behold how many thousands still are lying,
Bound in the darksome prison house of sin,
With none to tell them of the Savior's dying,
Or of the life He died for them to win.

Proclaim to every people, tongue, and nation
That God, in whom they live and move, is love;
Tell how He stooped to save His lost creation,
And died on earth that we might live above.

Give of thy sons to bear the message glorious;
Give of thy wealth to speed them on their way;
Pour out thy soul for them in prayer victorious;
And all thou spendest Jesus will repay.[3]

This song echoes God's Word, which says,

How beautiful upon the mountains are the feet of him
who brings good news, who publishes peace, who brings
good news of happiness, who publishes salvation, who
says to Zion, "Your God reigns" (Isa. 52:7).

Go therefore and make disciples of all nations, baptizing
them in the name of the Father and of the Son and of
the Holy Spirit, teaching them to observe all that I have
commanded you. And behold, I am with you always, to
the end of the age (Matt. 28:19-20).

Our God-given mandate is clear: Love much, send out.

ACTION POINTS

1. How has God encouraged or challenged you throughout the reading of this book?

   _____

   _____

   _____

   _____

2. How do you think successful parenting shows itself in a child?

   _____

   _____

   _____

   _____

3. What are some ways you can partner with your family to join God in His rescue mission?

   _____

   _____

   _____

   _____

A PERSONAL NOTE

On January 26, 2013, Esther and I were discussing our future dreams over some toasted turkey sandwiches at a local cafe. We were joking about selling our house, buying an RV, and traveling around the country ministering to small congregations by teaching parenting conferences. Our laughter turned the corner to excitement! "Let's write our own manual! If not for others, for our kids!" We quickly began brainstorming, jotting ideas all over a brown paper napkin while being entertained by an elderly woman sweetly playing "Amazing Grace" on the nearby piano.

It is only by this amazing grace that God has been our Guide, Constant Companion, and Guard. He has chosen to use us for His service and has now led us to write this book on parenting. There are so many milestones, ministries, books, and people that have molded our convictions on this topic. We are writing with humility and gratitude knowing that we made, and will continue to make, many mistakes. BUT GOD in His grace continues to bring beauty from the ashes of our lives.

We have quoted 3 John 1:4 several times throughout this manuscript: "I have no greater joy than to hear that my children are walking in the truth." This life verse is both the motivation and reward in parenting as well as a comrade in combat for the good of our children, the sake of our joy, and the glory of our God.

THANK YOU to our children, family, students, and friends for being our balcony people, cheering us on! Special thanks also to:

Casey Cease, Lucid Books CEO and good friend long before his involvement with book publishing. For his gracious support and encouragement to a couple of rookie writers.

Jim and Bonnie Huntington, long-time friends whose North Carolina mountain cabin became our sanctuary of prayer and brainstorming for this book.

Lei Ann Carson, friend and proofreader. There is absolutely no way to adequately express the extent to which she went to provide such expert advice and guidance which was so desperately needed. Truly a gracious gift from God and one of the many sources of confirmation, albeit in a class all its own, regarding our mission to write this book.

I would also like to express our deep appreciation to Dr. Stephen Rummage and Bell Shoals Baptist Church for their ministry investment and partnership in helping us raise and release our three arrow-children.

RECOMMENDED READING

There are so many great books that have been written on the topic of marriage and family. The following list is just a few that we endorse and that were helpful in writing this book:

Shadow of the Almighty: The Life and Testament of Jim Elliot, by Elisabeth Elliot

Let the Nations Be Glad!: The Supremacy of God in Missions, by John Piper

You and Me Forever: Marriage in Light of Eternity, by Francis and Lisa Chan

Revolutionary Parenting, by George Barna

Gospel-Powered Parenting, by William Farley

Give Them Grace: Dazzling Your Kids with the Love of Jesus, by Elyse M. Fitzpatrick and Jessica Thompson

ApParent Privilege, by Steve and Tina Wright

The Sticky Faith Guide for your Family, by Dr. Kara E. Powell

The Faithful Parent, by Martha Peace and Stewart Scott

Parenting with Scripture, by Kara Durbin

Leaving the Light On, by Gary Smalley and John Trent

Raising a Modern Day Knight: A Father's Role in Guiding His Son to Authentic Manhood, by Robert Lewis

She Calls Me Daddy: 7 Things You Need to Know About Building a Complete Daughter, by Robert Wolgemuth

Growing Up: How to be a Disciple Who Makes Disciples, by Robby Gallaty

NOTES

Introduction

1. Elisabeth Elliot, *Shadow of the Almighty: The Life and Testament of Jim Elliot* (New York: Harper, 1958), 132.

2. John Piper, "Raising Children Who Are Confident in God," Desiring God, February 25, 1996, accessed August 3, 2015, www.desiringgod.org/ sermons/ raising-children-who-are-confident-in-god.

Chapter 1: Upholding the Cause of the King

1. *Baker's Evangelical Dictionary of Biblical Theology*, ed. Walter A. Elwell (Grand Rapids: Baker Books, 1996), quoted in "Mission," BibleStudyTools.com, accessed August 3, 2015, www.biblestudytools.com/ dictionaries/bakers-evangelical-dictionary/mission. html.

Chapter 2: Identifying the Target

1. C. S. Lewis, *The Chronicles of Narnia: The Last Battle* (New York: Scholastic Inc., 1995), 210-11.

2. Tyler D. Flores, "The Gospel: The Glorious Impact between the Holy and the Dead," *Keeping the Son in my Eyes*, (blog), July 31, 2010, accessed August 3, 2015, https://tflores. wordpress.com/ 2010/07/31/ the-gospel-the-glorious-impact-between-the-holy-and-the-dead/KeepingtheSoninmyeyes.

3. Matthew Henry, "Psalms 127," Biblestudytools. com, accessed August 11, 2015, http://www. biblestudytools.com/commentaries/matthew-henry-complete/psalms/127.html.

Chapter 3: Establishing a Foundation

1. Steve Green, "Household of Faith," 1985.

2. C. S. Lewis, *Beyond Personality* (New York: The Macmillan Company, 1947), 40.

3. Charles Spurgeon, E-word Today.com, accessed August 11, 2015, https://www.ewordtoday.com/ spurgeon/0122am.htm.

4. Edward Mote, "My Hope is Built," 1834.

5. Spurgeon, "Psalm 127," The Spurgeon Archive, accessed August 11, 2015, www.spurgeon.org/ treasury/ps127.htm.

Chapter 4: Conforming my Heart

1. Ruth Bell Graham, *It's My Turn: Life Lessons From the Wife of Billy Graham* (Old Tappan, NJ: Revell, 1932), 74.

2. Walter Wangerin, Jr., *As For Me and My House: Crafting Your Marriage to Last* (Nashville: Thomas Nelson Publishers, 1987), 79-80.

3. Judson W. Van DeVenter, "I Surrender All," 1896.

Chapter 5: Fashioning the Arrows

1. "Bow and Arrow," Encyclopedia Britannica, accessed August 11, 2015, www.britannica.com/technology/bow-and-arrow.

2. Elliot, *Shadow of the Almighty*, 132.

3. Joni Eareckson Tada, "Steve Saint," Joni and Friends: International Disability Center, accessed August 11, 2015, www.joniandfriends.org/radio/5-minute/steve-saint.

4. "Fletching Guide," Trueflight Feathers, accessed August 11, 2015, www.trueflightfeathers.com/guide.htm.

5. Jim Putman and Bobby Harrington, *Discipleshift: Five Steps That Help Your Church to Make Disciples Who Make Disciples* (Grand Rapids: Zondervan Publishing House, 2013), 120.

Chapter 6: Guarding the Deposit

1. Dr. James Dobson, "Power Games," Dr. James Dobson's familytalk, accessed August 11, 2015, http://drjamesdobson.org/articles/protect-and-defend/power-games.

Chapter 7: Directing their Path

1. Matthew Henry, *Commentary on the Whole Bible Volume I (Genesis to Deuteronomy)*, quoted in Christian Classics Ethereal Library, accessed August 15, 2015, http://www.ccel.org/ccel/henry/mhc1.Deu.vii.html.

2. John Piper, "The Weapon Serves the Wielding Power," Desiring God, accessed August 11, 2015,

http://www.desiringgod.org/messages/the-weapon-serves-the-wielding-power.

3. Trevin Wax, "Jim Elliot's Brother, Bert: The Hero You Don't Know," The Gospel Coalition, (blog), October 9, 2013, accessed August 15, 2015, http://www.the-gospelcoalition.org/blogs/trevinwax/2013/10/09/jim-elliots-brother-bert-the-hero-you-dont-know/.

Chapter 8: Releasing with Intention

1. Mrs. Catherine Jane Filson Carmichael, quoted in Elisabeth Elliot, *A Chance to Die: the Life and Legacy of Amy Carmichael* (New Jersey: Fleming H. Revell Company, 1987), 55.

2. Elliot, *Shadow of the Almighty*, 132.

3. Mary Ann Faulkner Thomson, "O Zion, Haste," 1868.

CPSIA information can be obtained at www.ICGtesting.com
Printed in the USA
LVOW10s0501020316

477404LV00003B/3/P